Beautiful Brides

GRAYSCALE COLORING BOOK

Bibliographical Note
Beautiful Brides Coloring Book is a new work,
first published by Amazon, Inc, in 2023

International Standard Book Number
ISBN: 9798870618357

Manufactured in US

"Step into the enchanting world of timeless romance with our exquisite adult coloring book, 'Beautiful Brides.' Immerse yourself in the artistry of love as you bring to life stunning portraits of a beautiful bride adorned in a classic wedding dress that transcends eras.

Each page of this captivating coloring book showcases the grace and sophistication of the bride, her features captured in realistic detail, allowing you to explore the nuances of expression and emotion. The focal point, however, is the breathtaking wedding gown- a masterpiece of elegance and refinement.

Draped in the finest grayscale tones, the intricacies of the lace detailing on the gown come alive under your creative touch. As you navigate through the pages, you'll discover the flowing veil that cascades with ethereal beauty, creating an aura of romance and timelessness. The grayscale palette enhances the realism, offering a unique and sophisticated coloring experience that allows you to play with shadows, highlights, and texture.

Indulge your artistic sensibilities and bring out the subtle nuances of the bride's attire, from the delicate lace patterns to the gentle folds of the dress. This adult coloring book is a celebration of the enduring charm of a classic wedding ensemble, offering a meditative and joyful escape into the world of bridal elegance.

Whether you're a coloring enthusiast, a bride-to-be seeking inspiration, or someone captivated by the allure of timeless fashion, 'Beautiful Brides' invites you to embark on a coloring journey that combines creativity, beauty, and the everlasting magic of a bride in her most splendid moment."

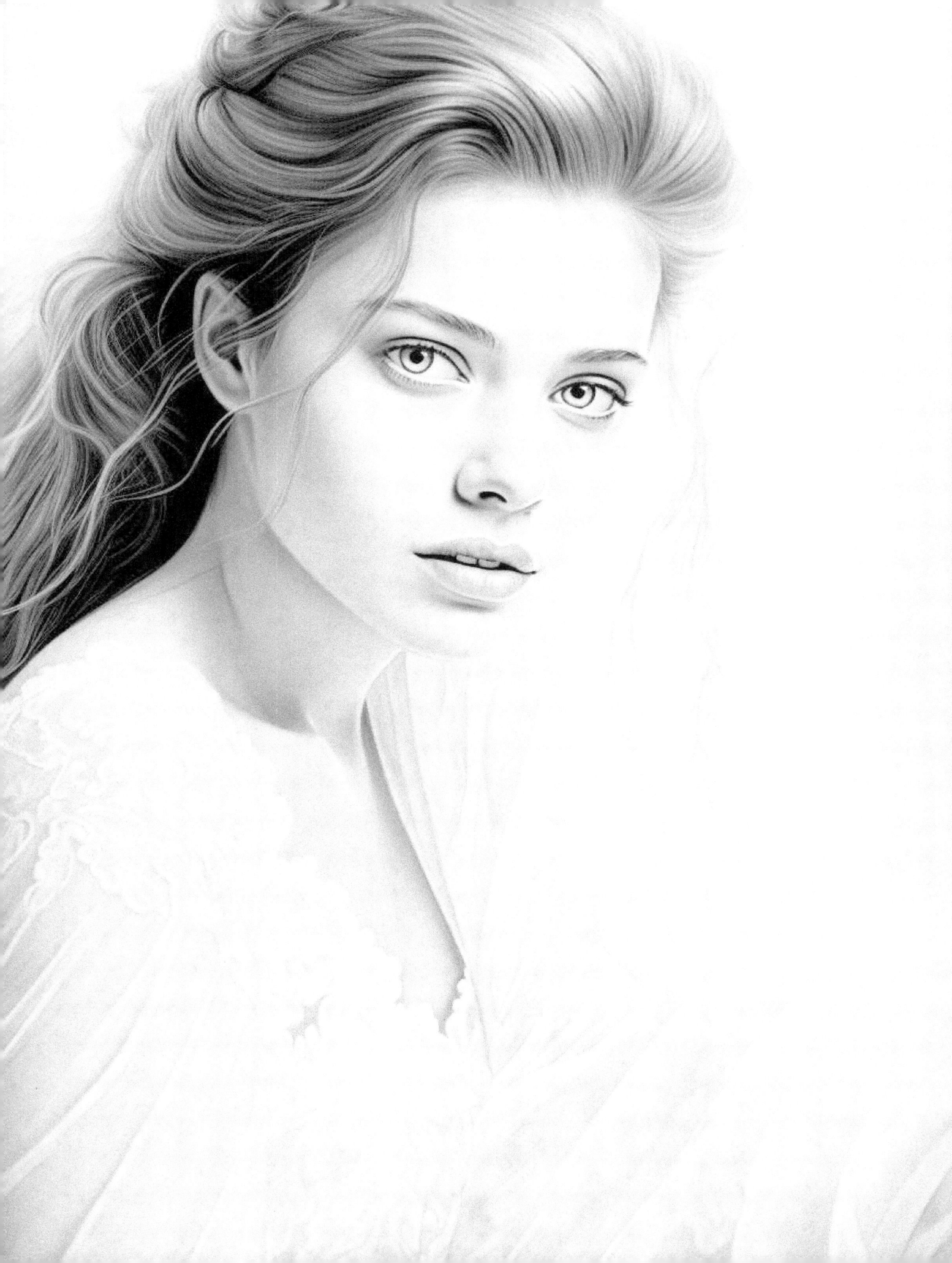

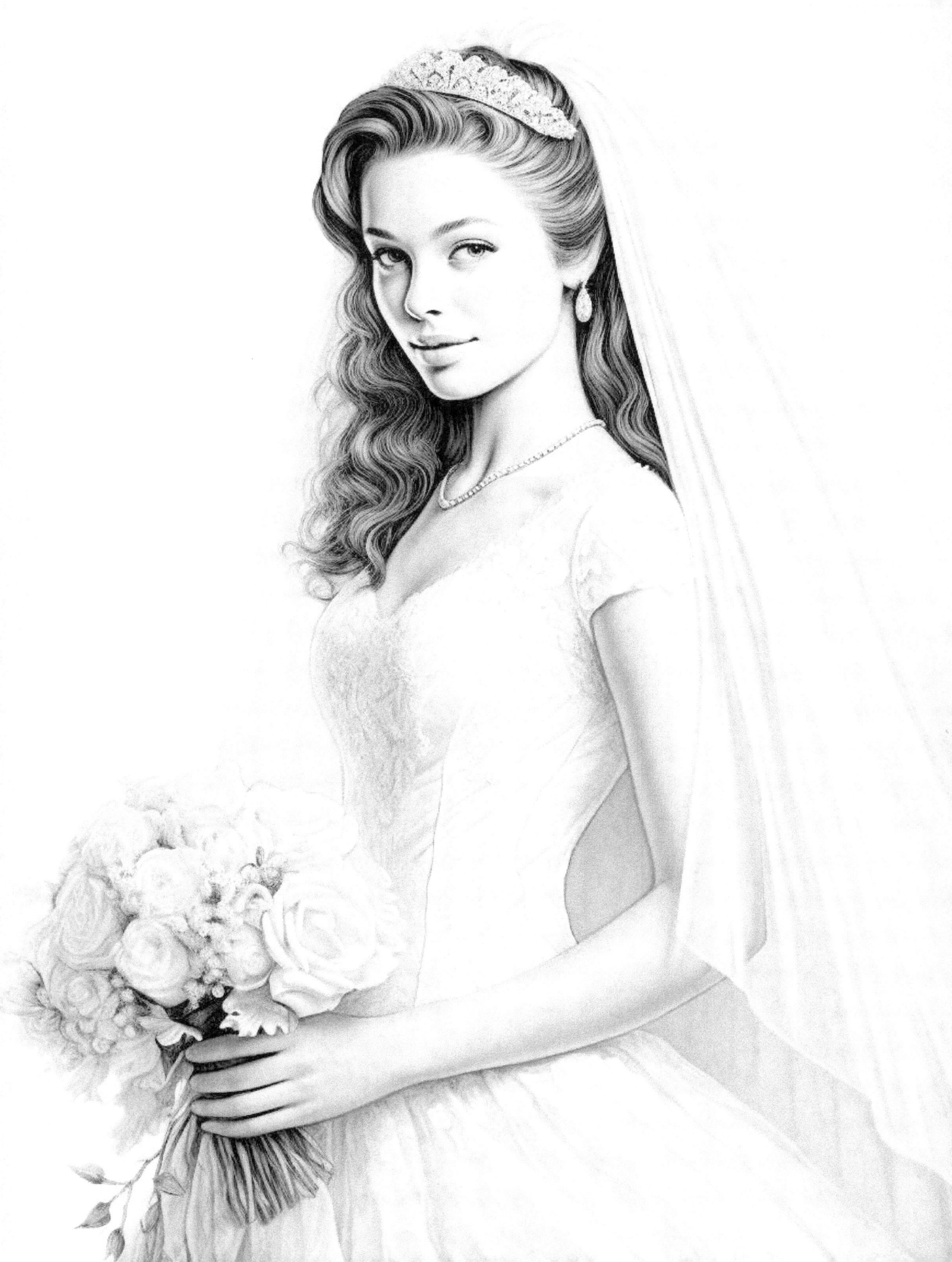

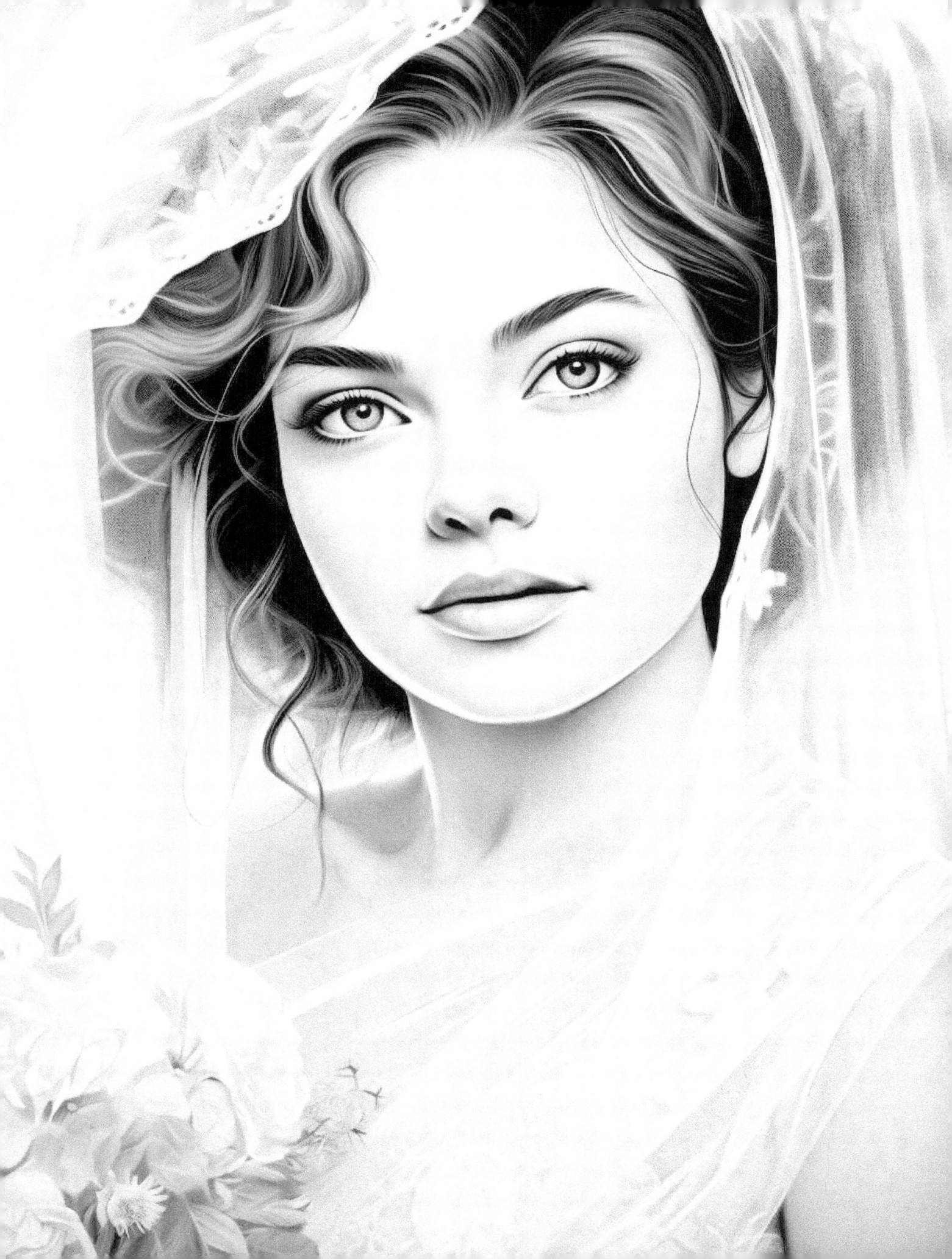

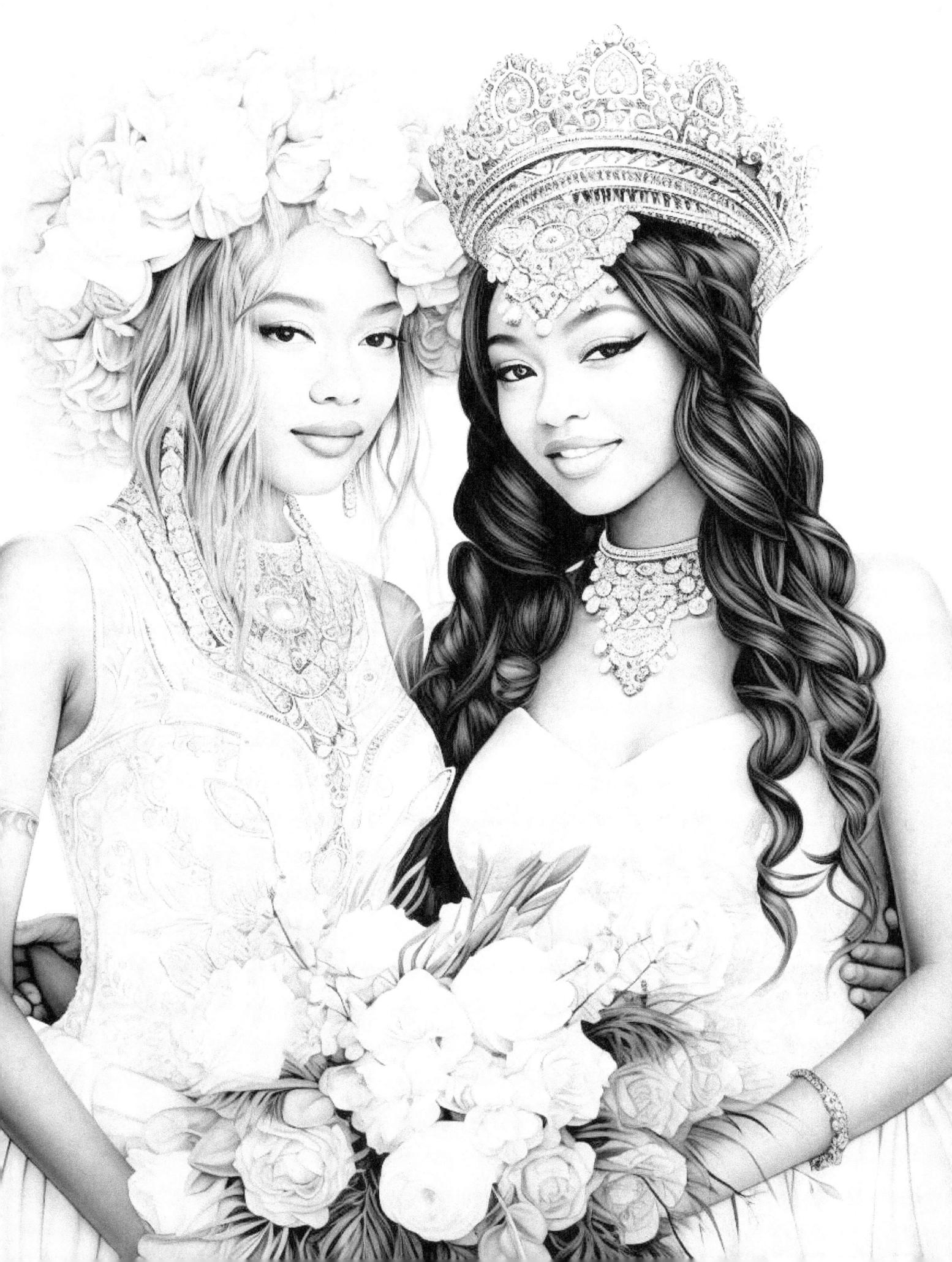

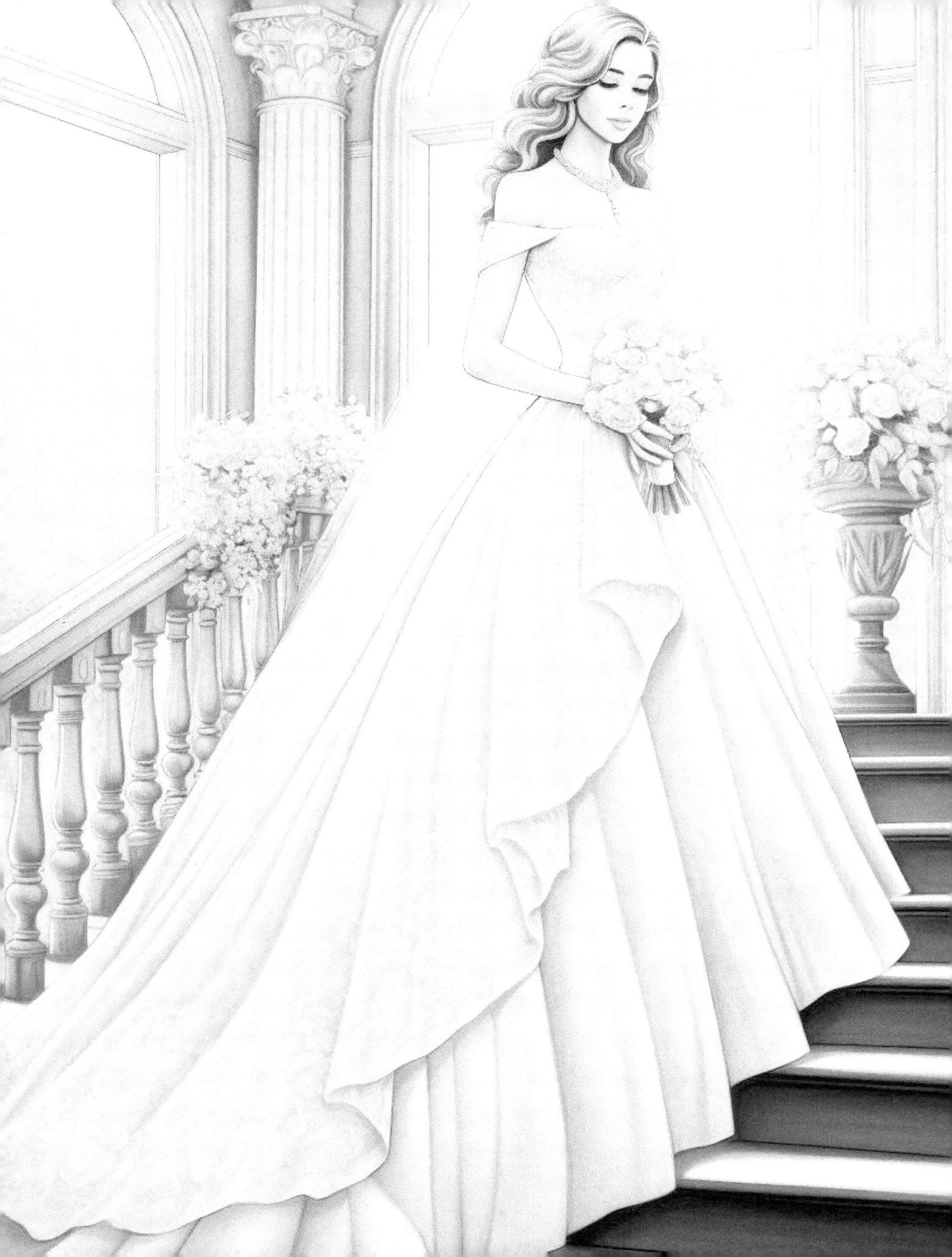

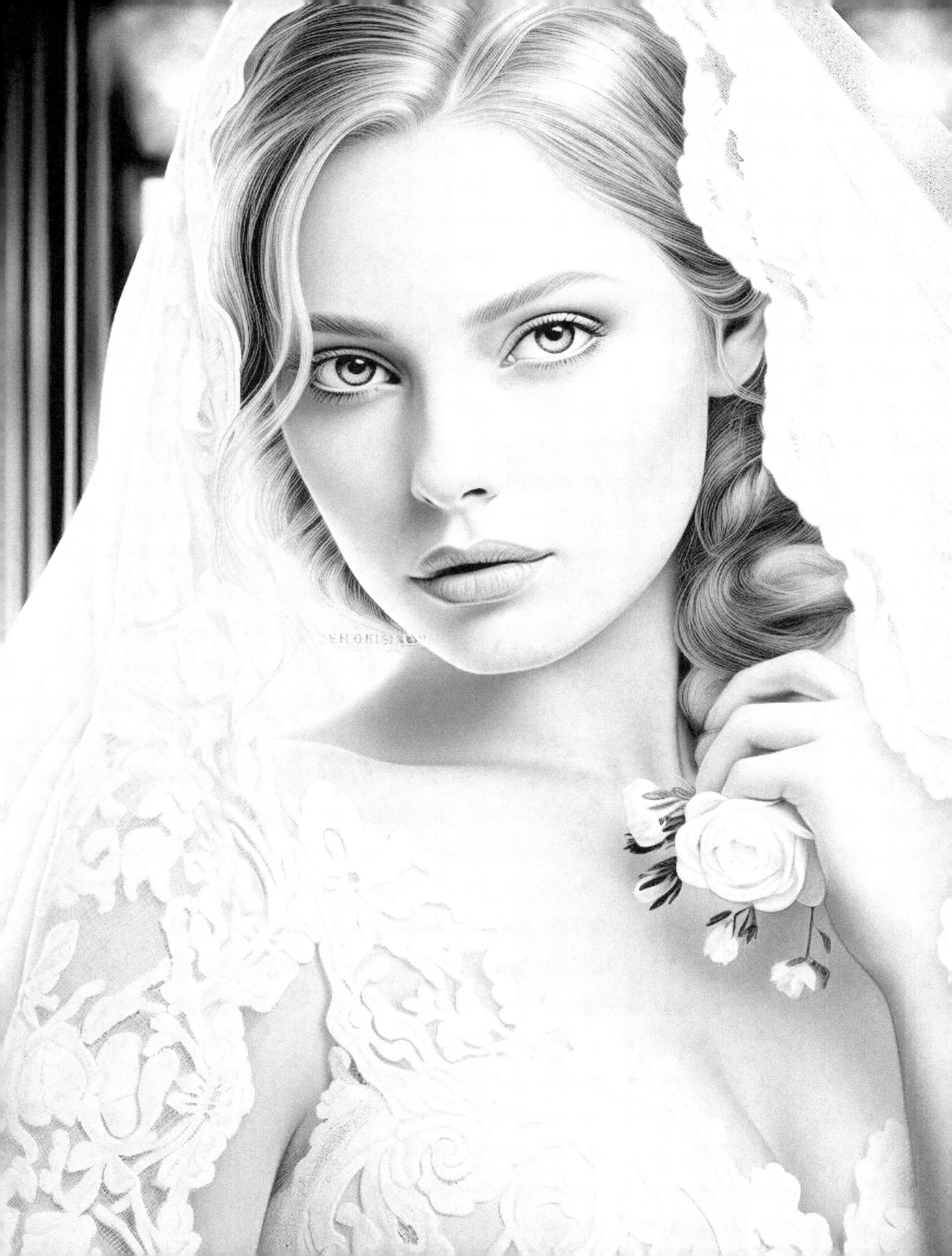

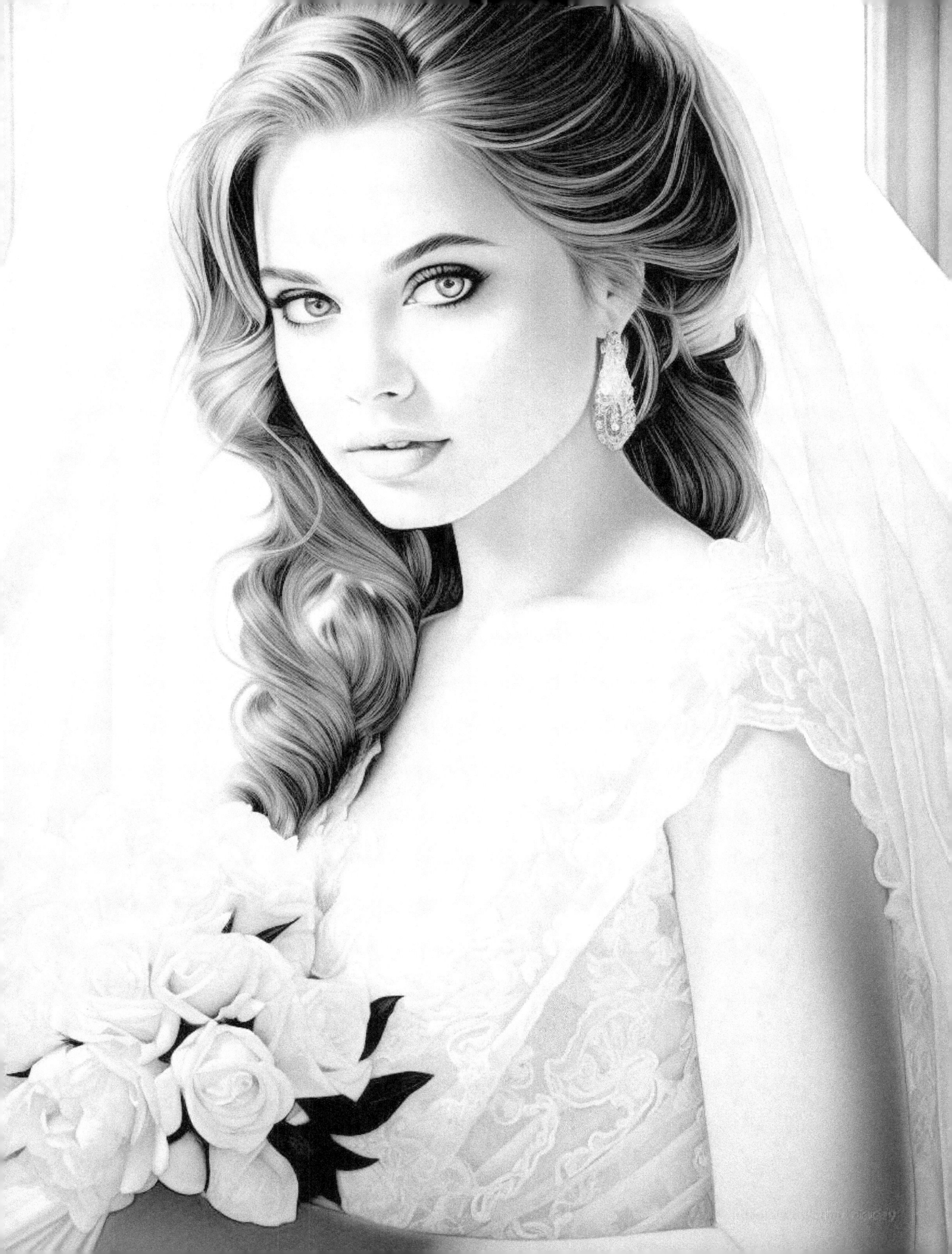

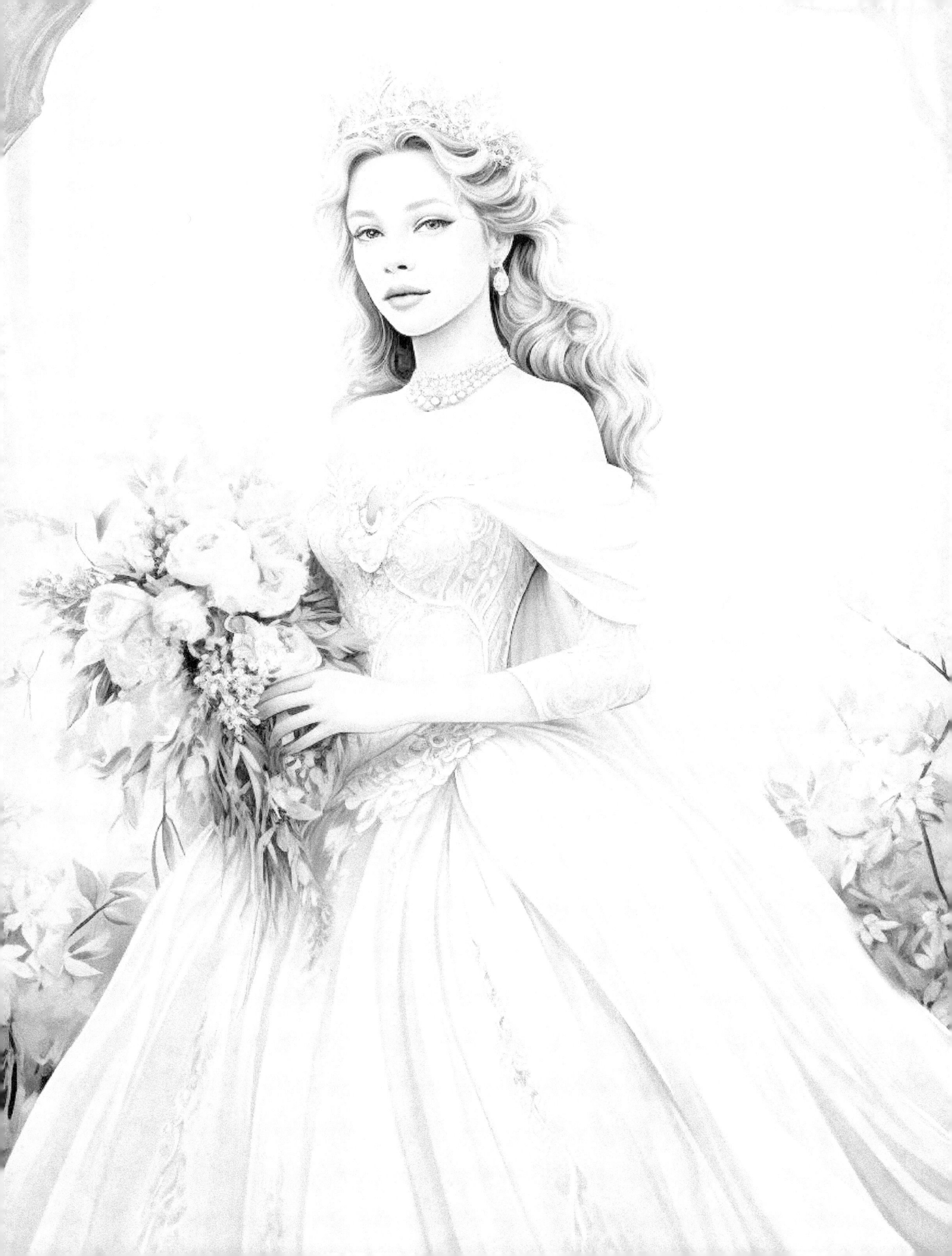

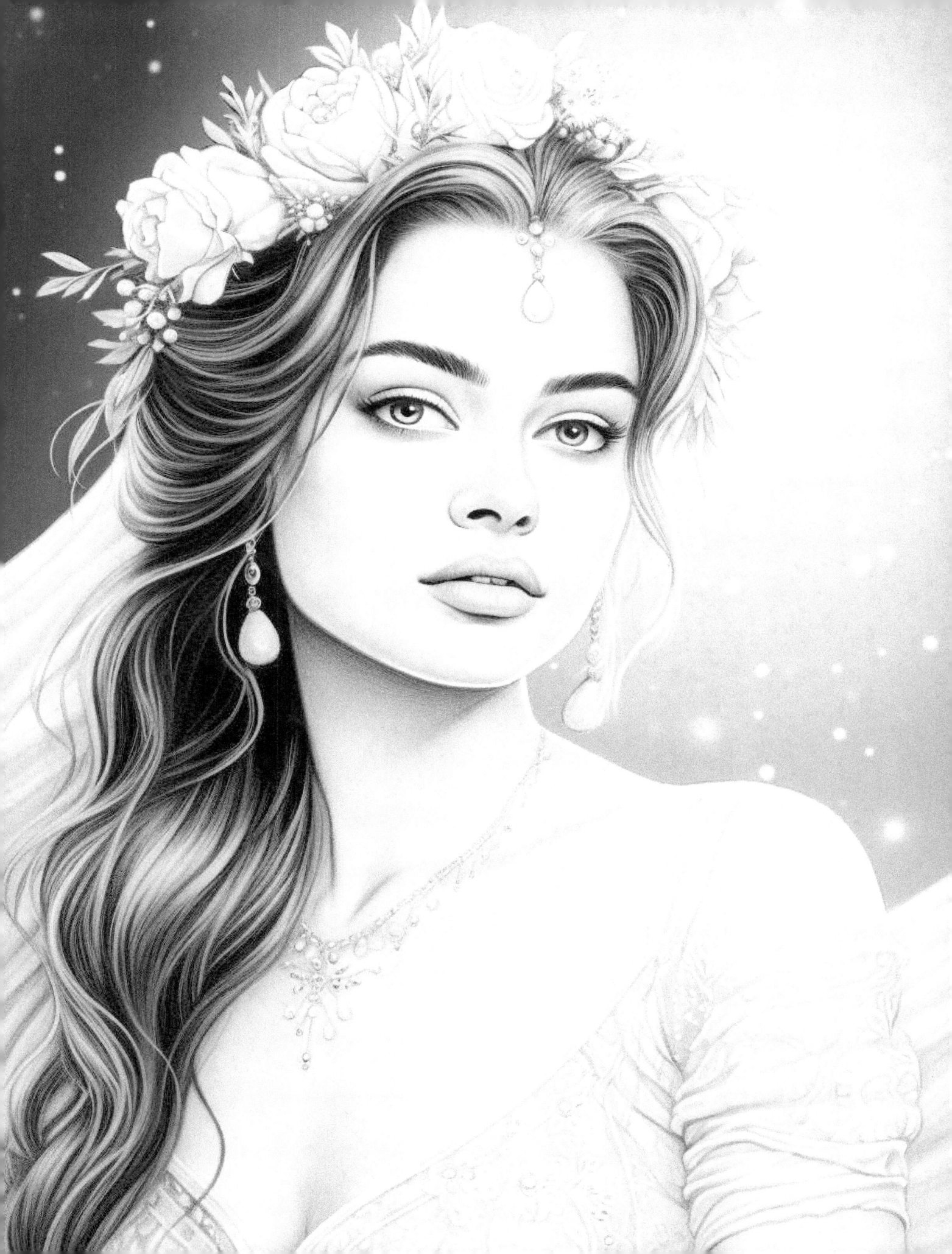

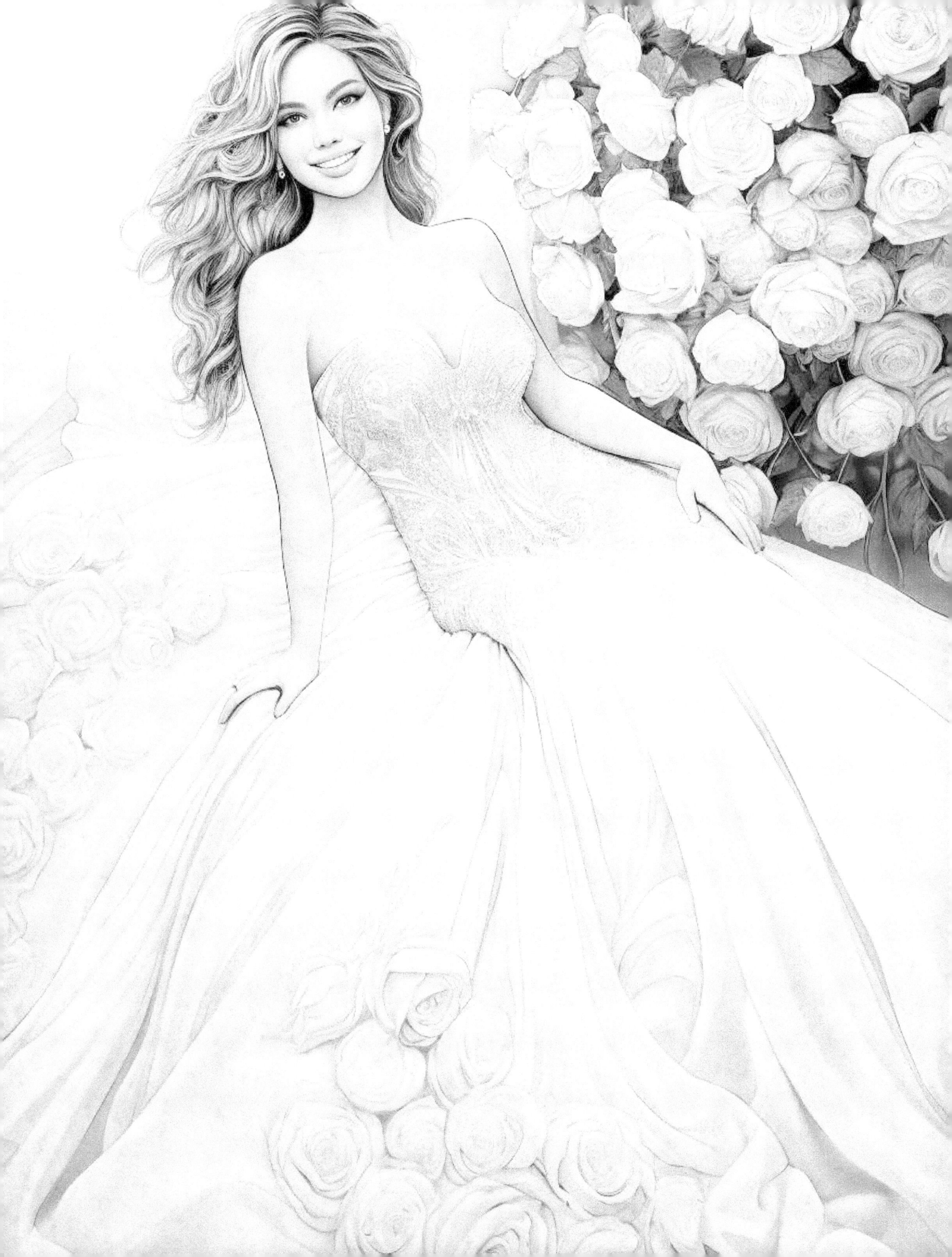

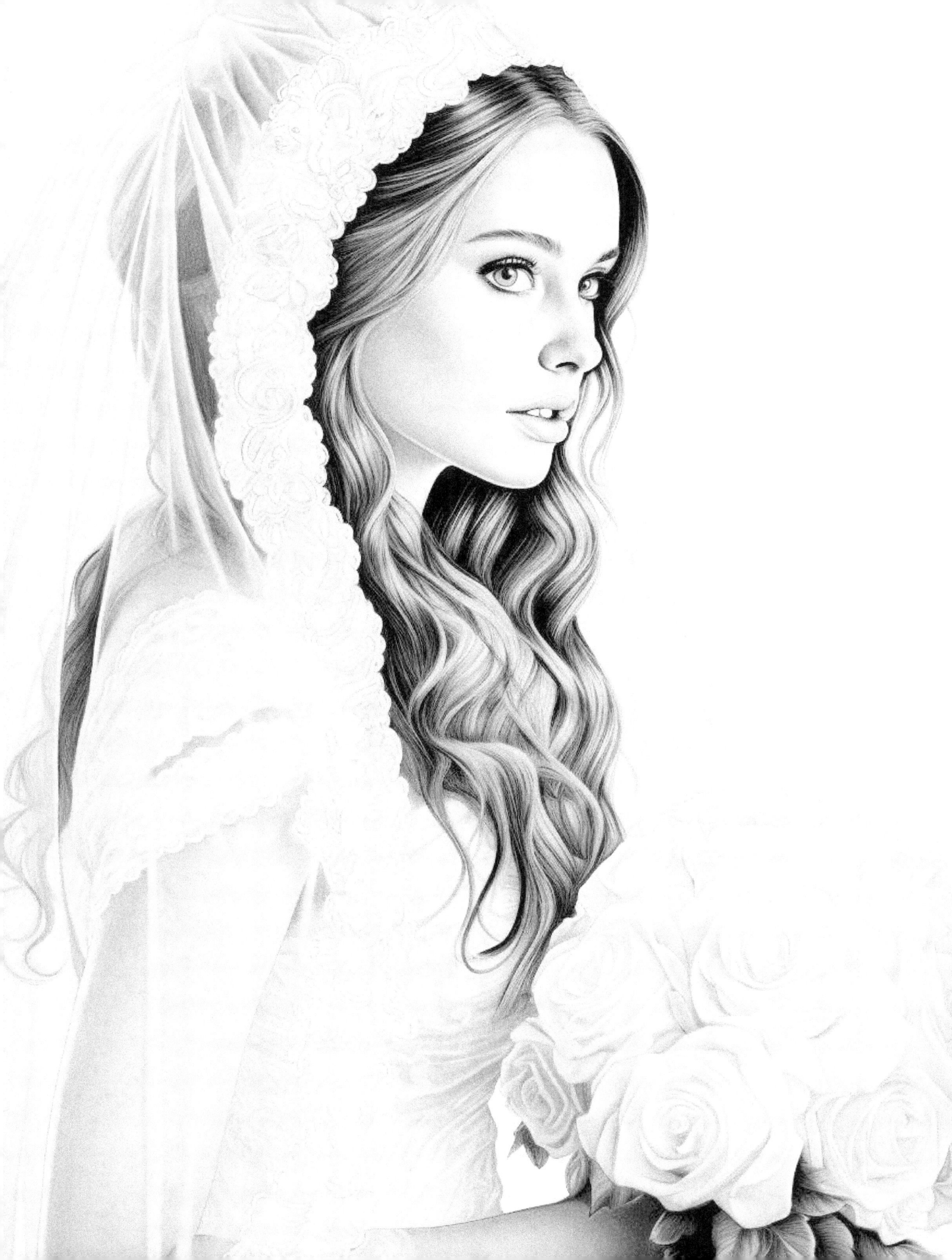

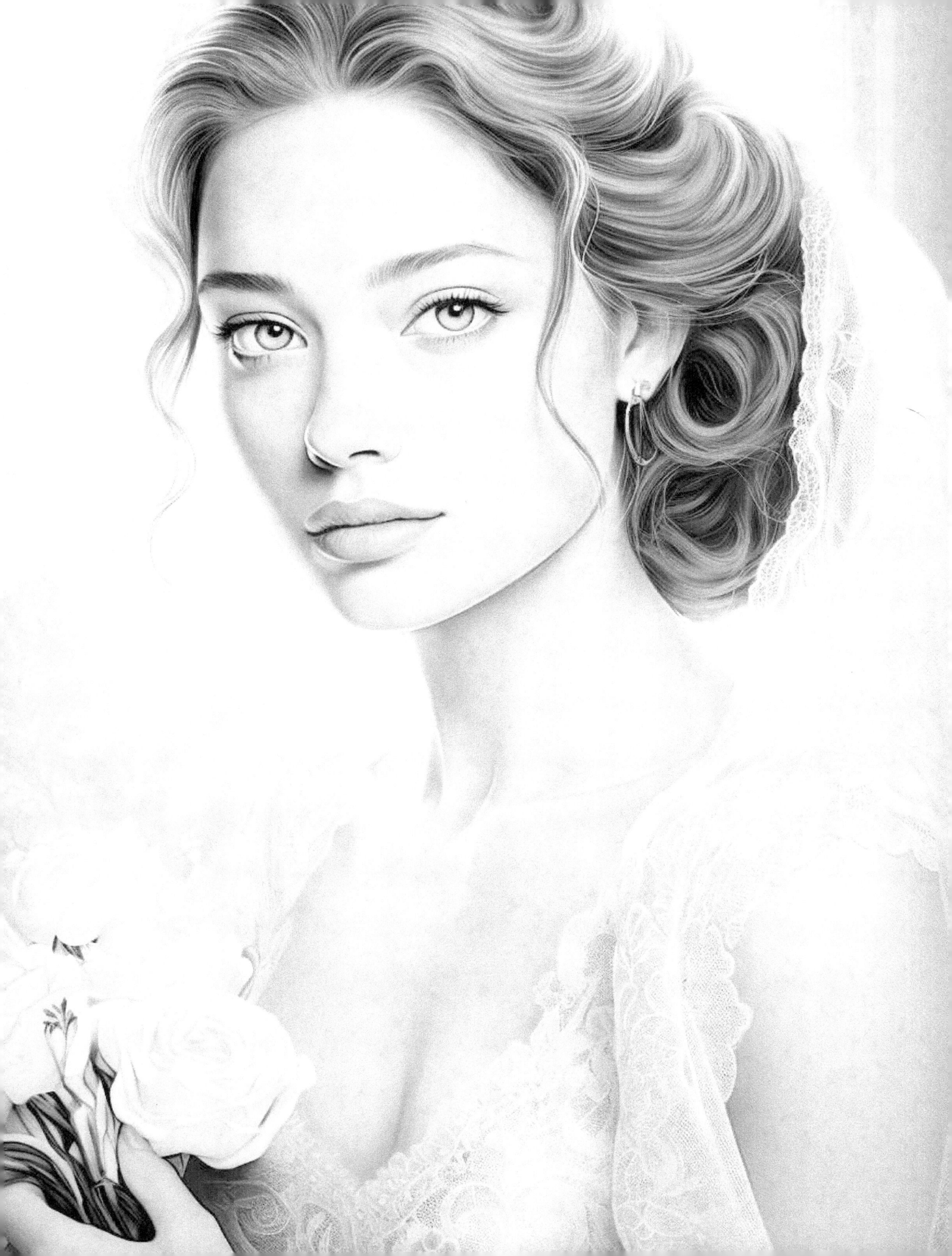

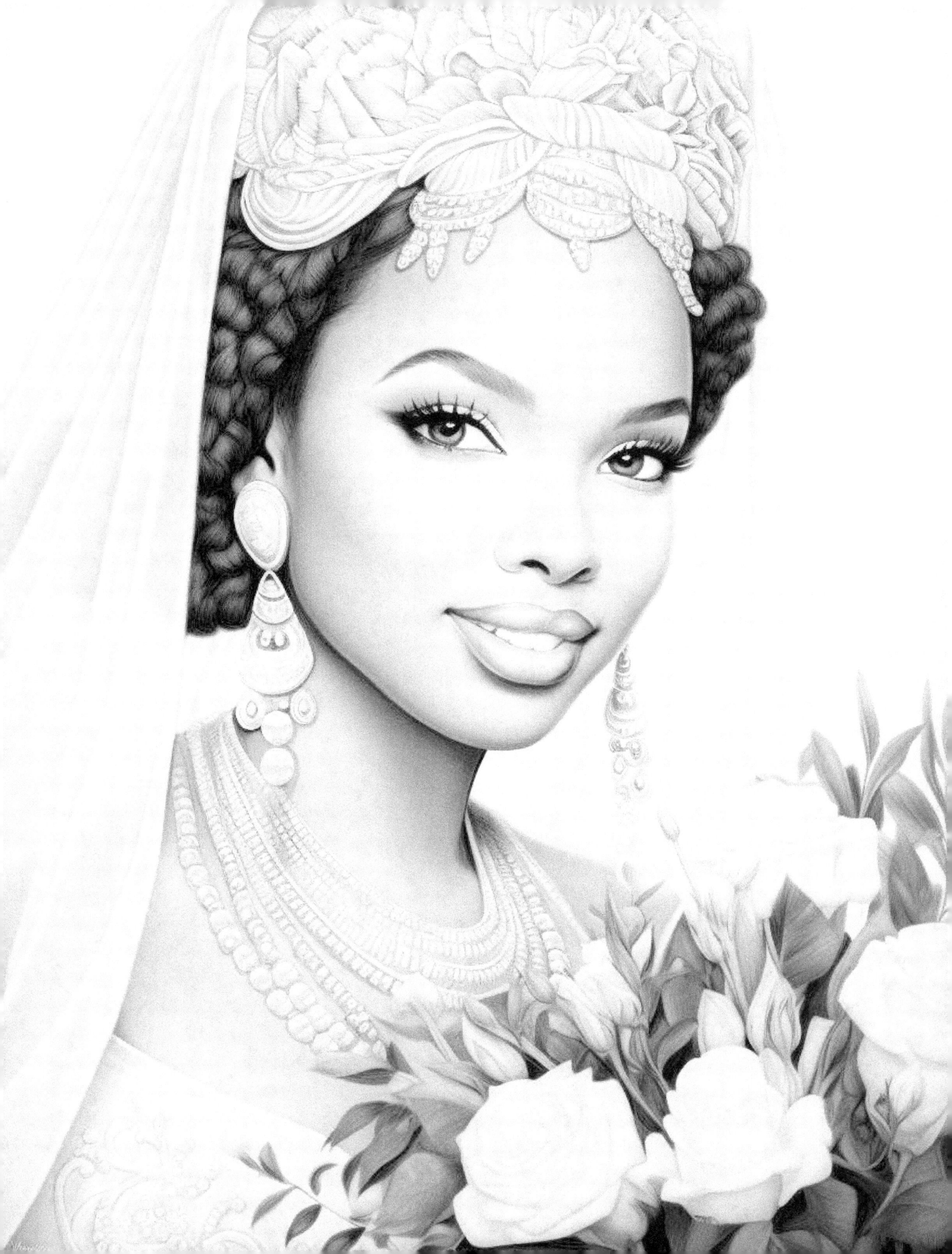

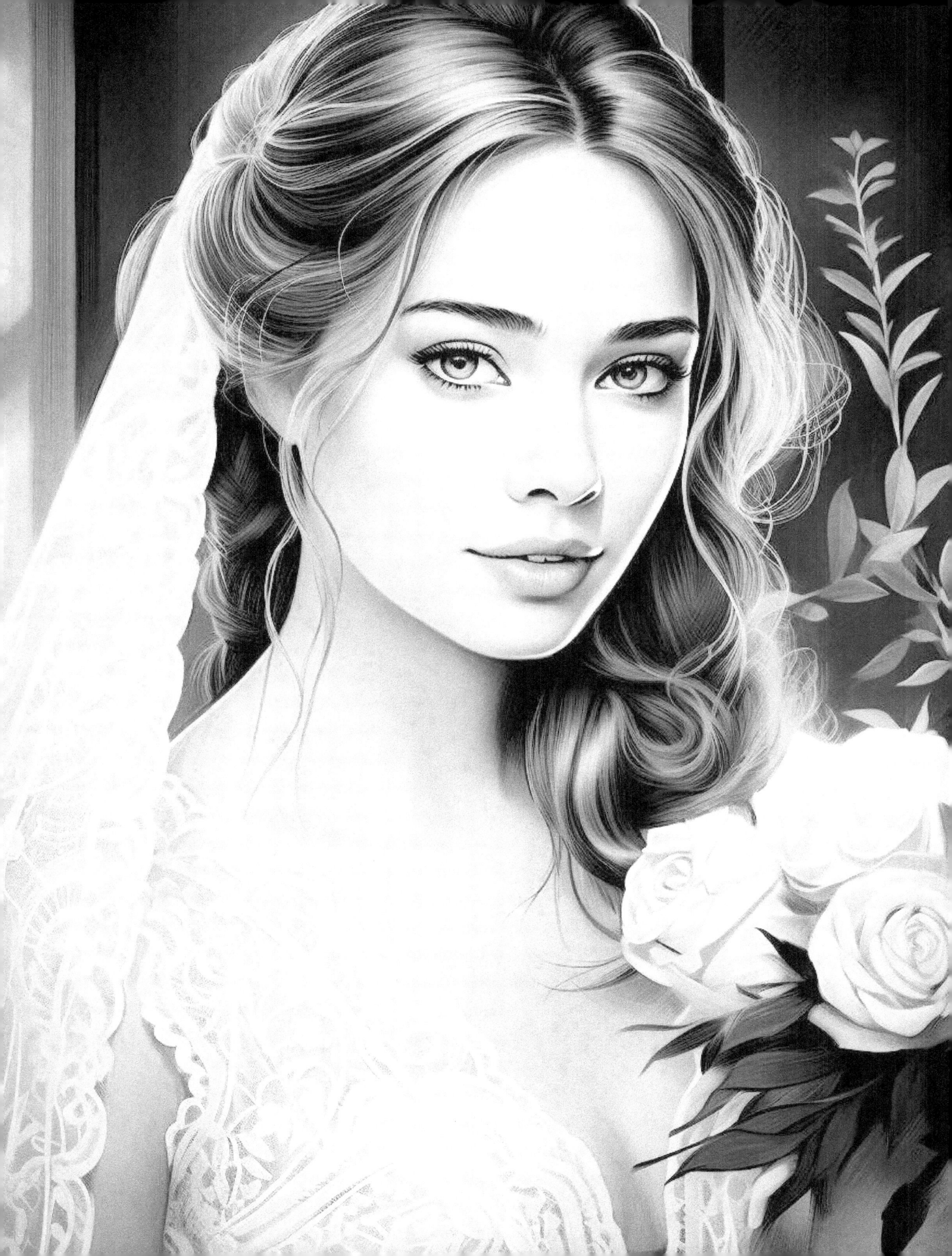

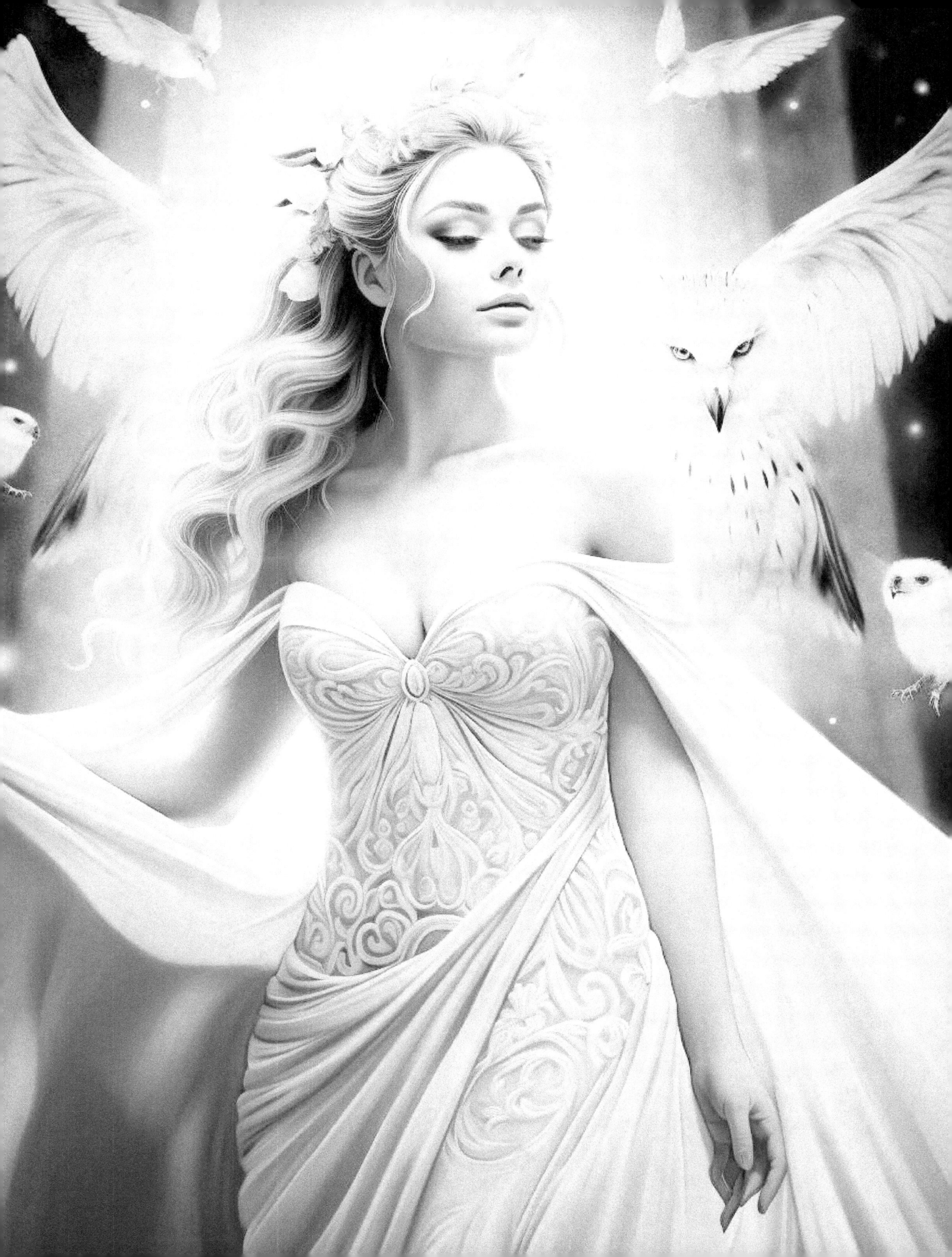

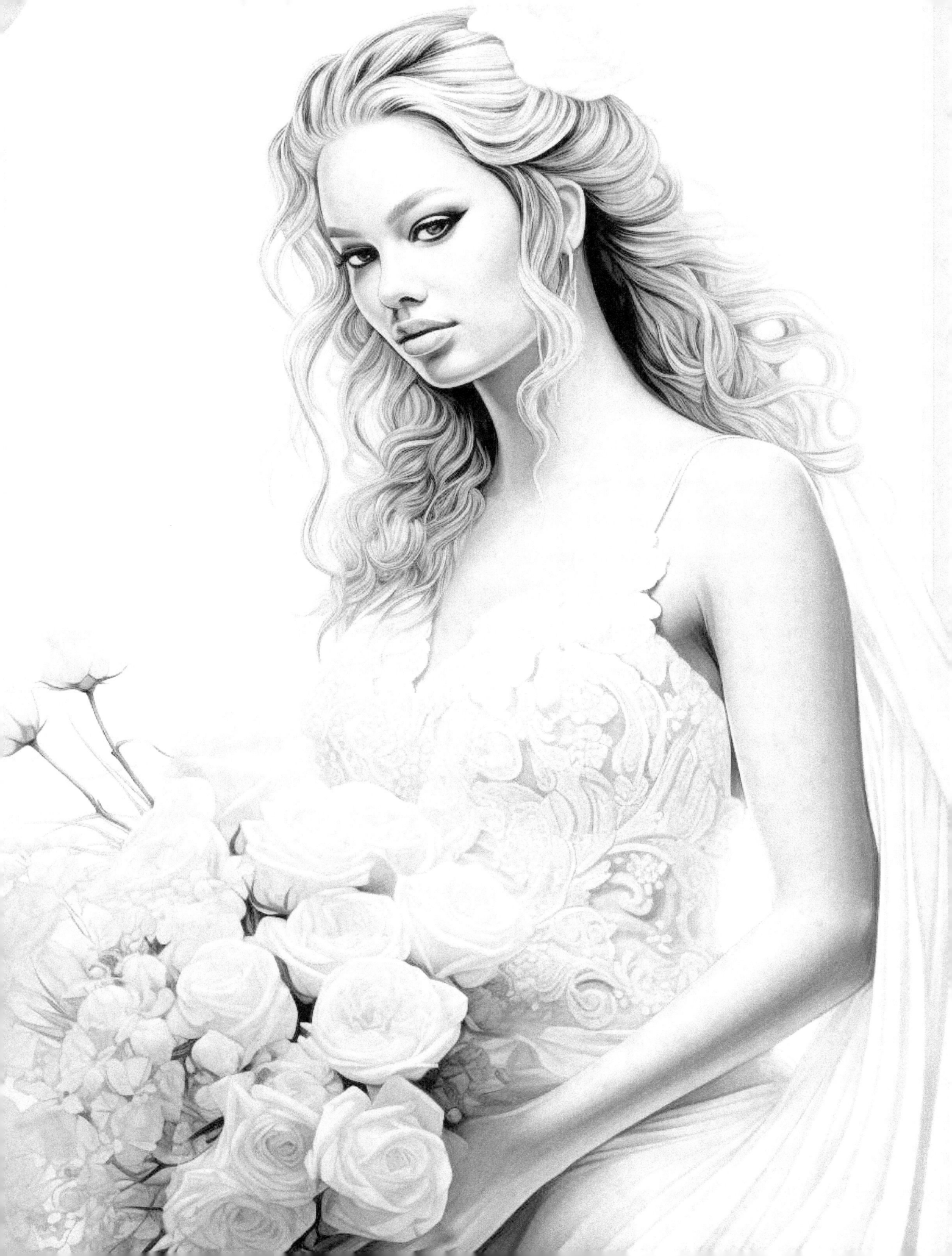

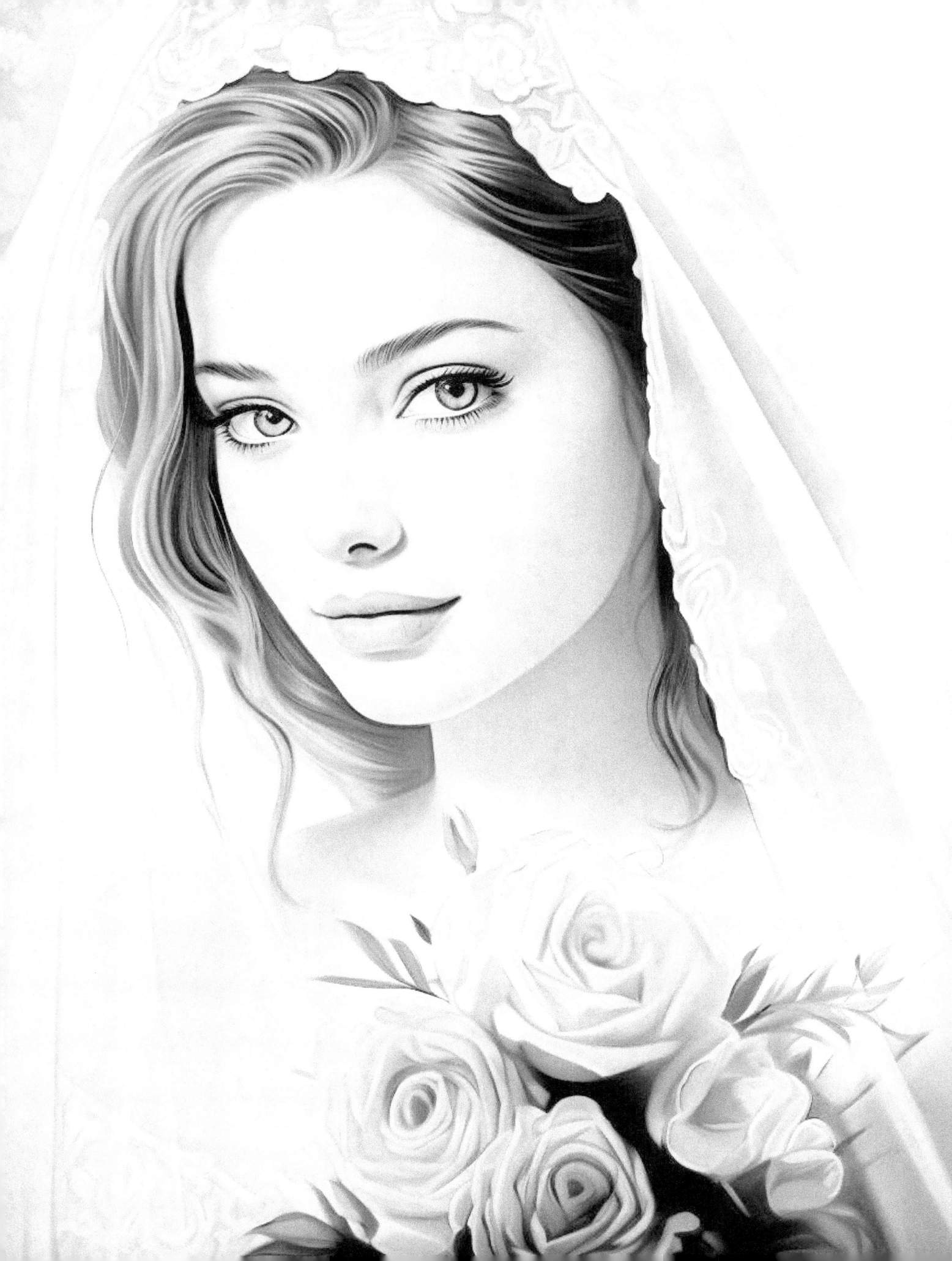

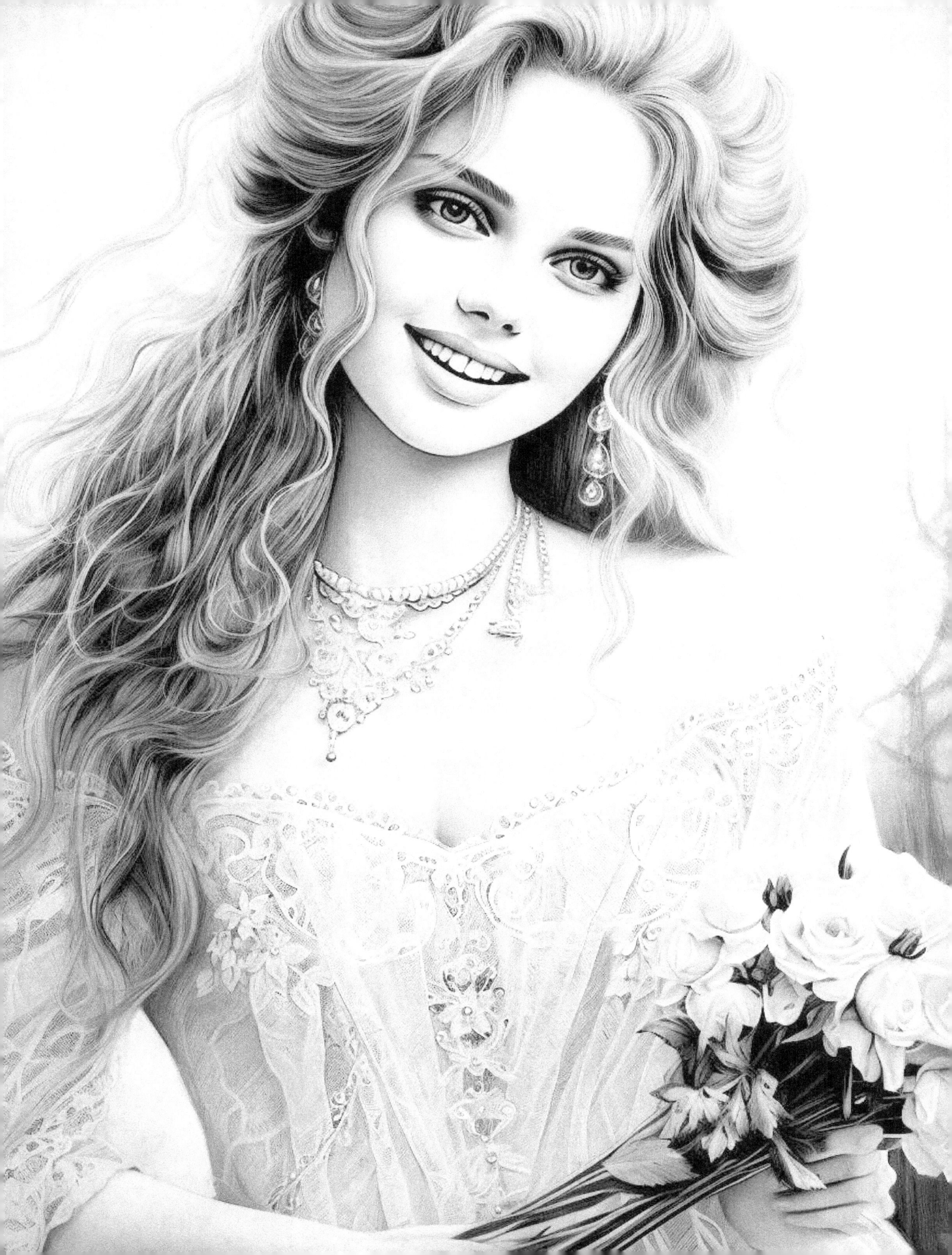

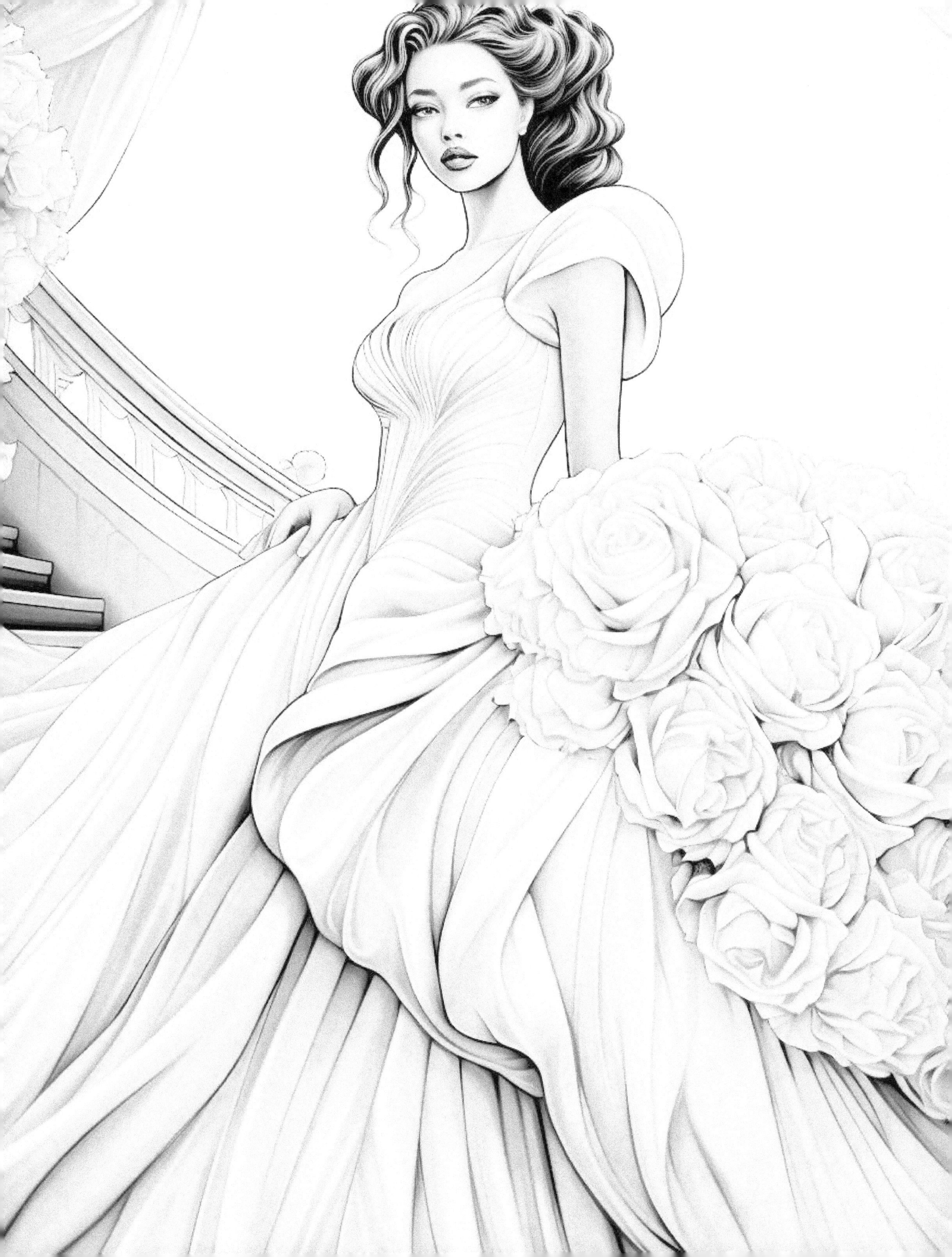

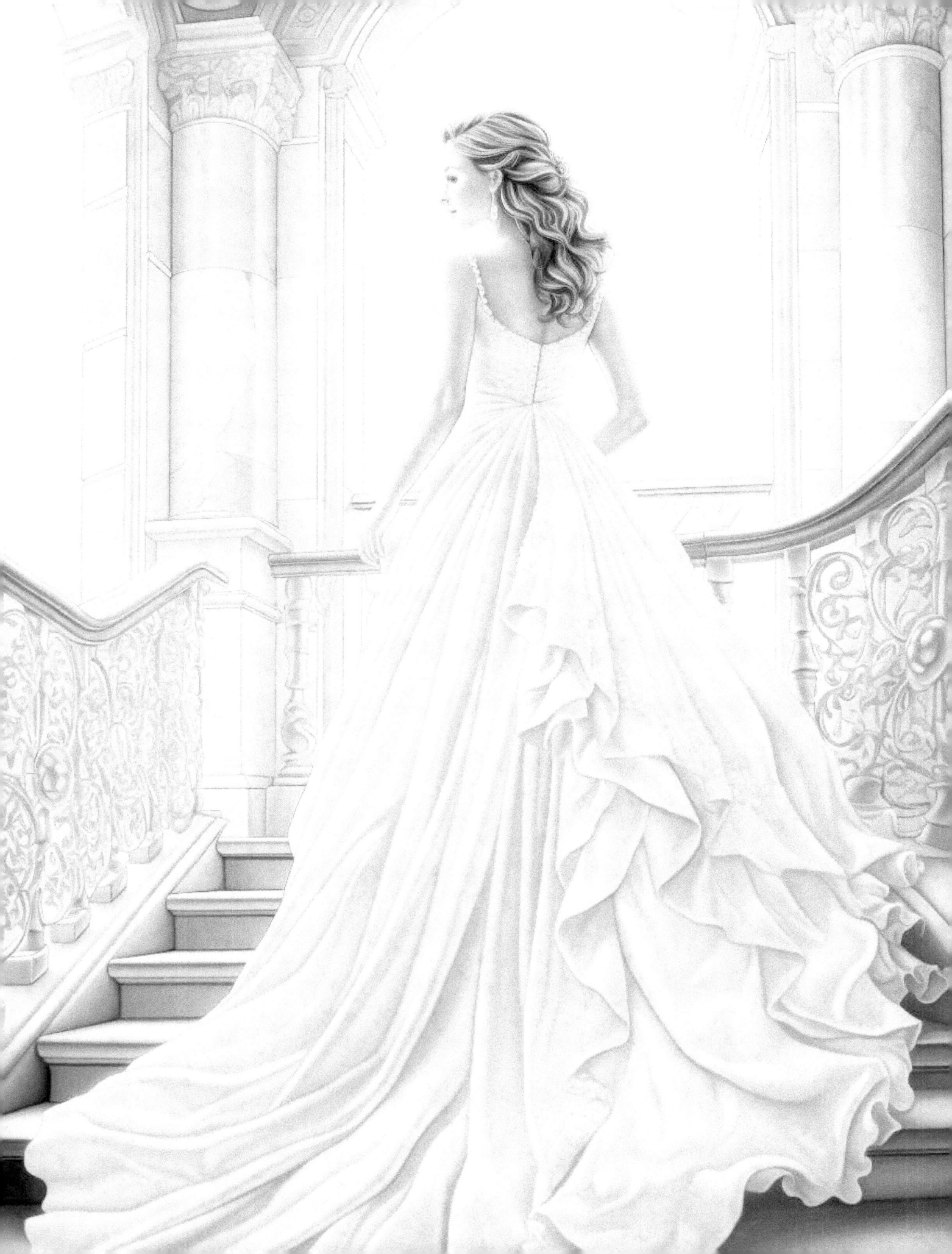

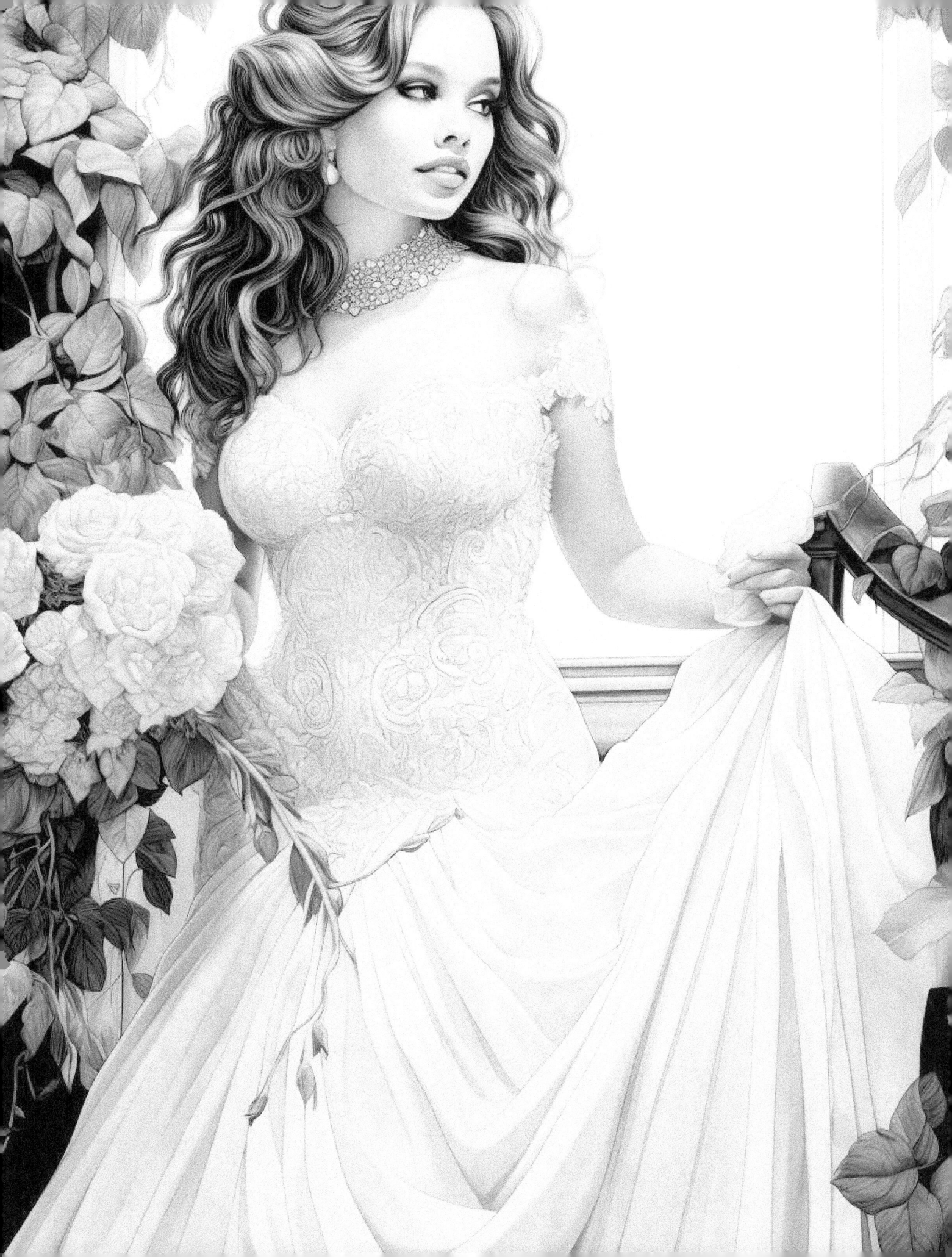

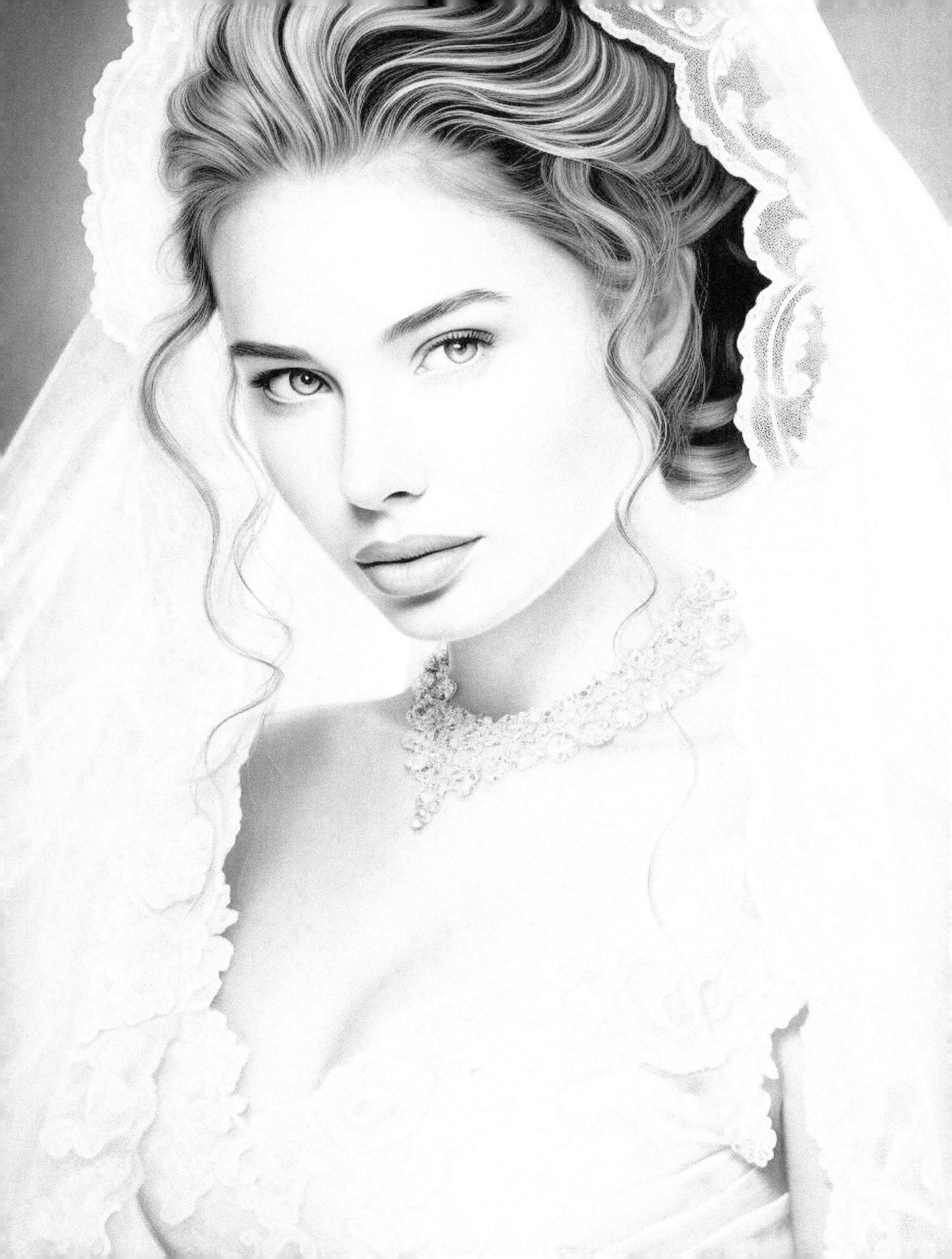

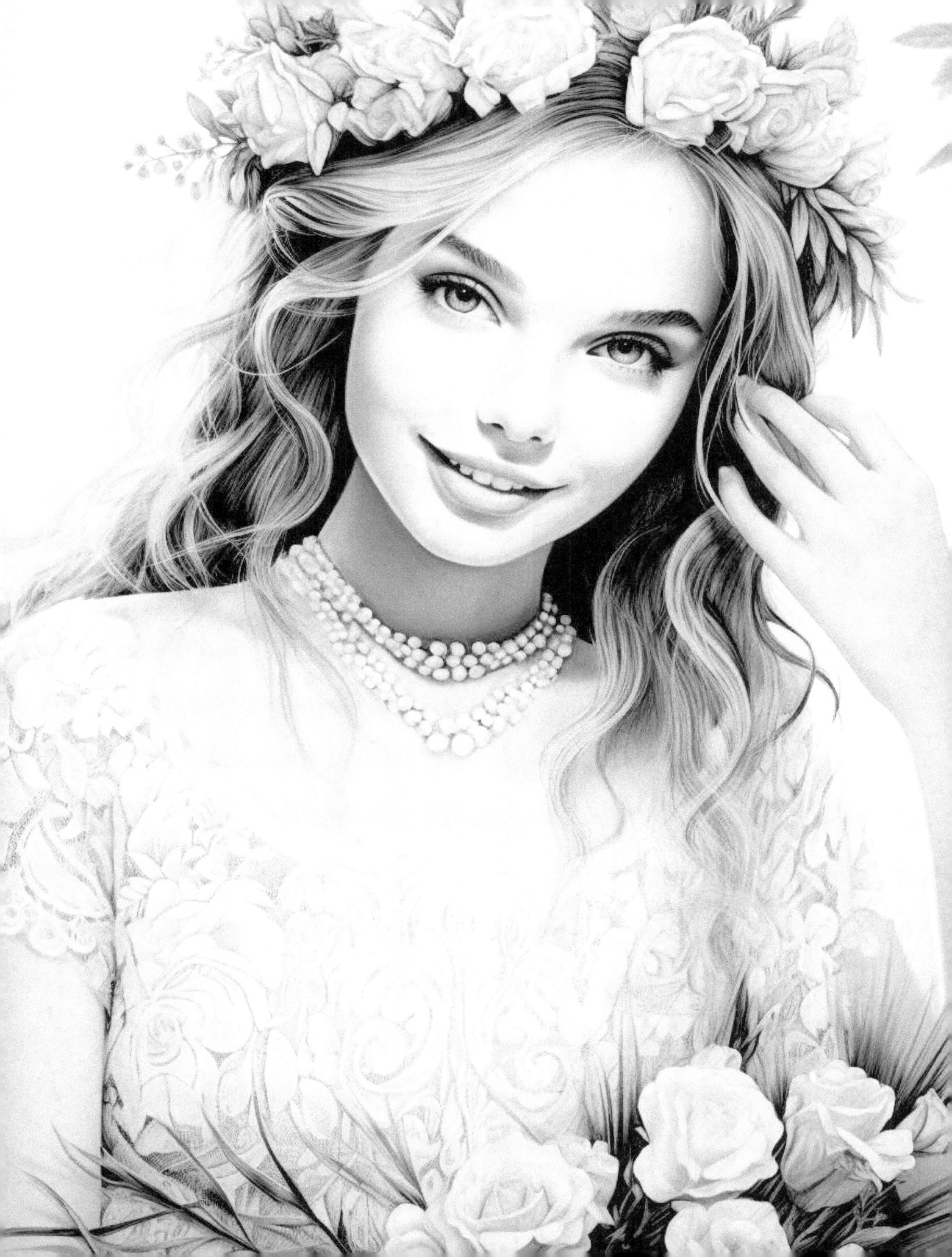

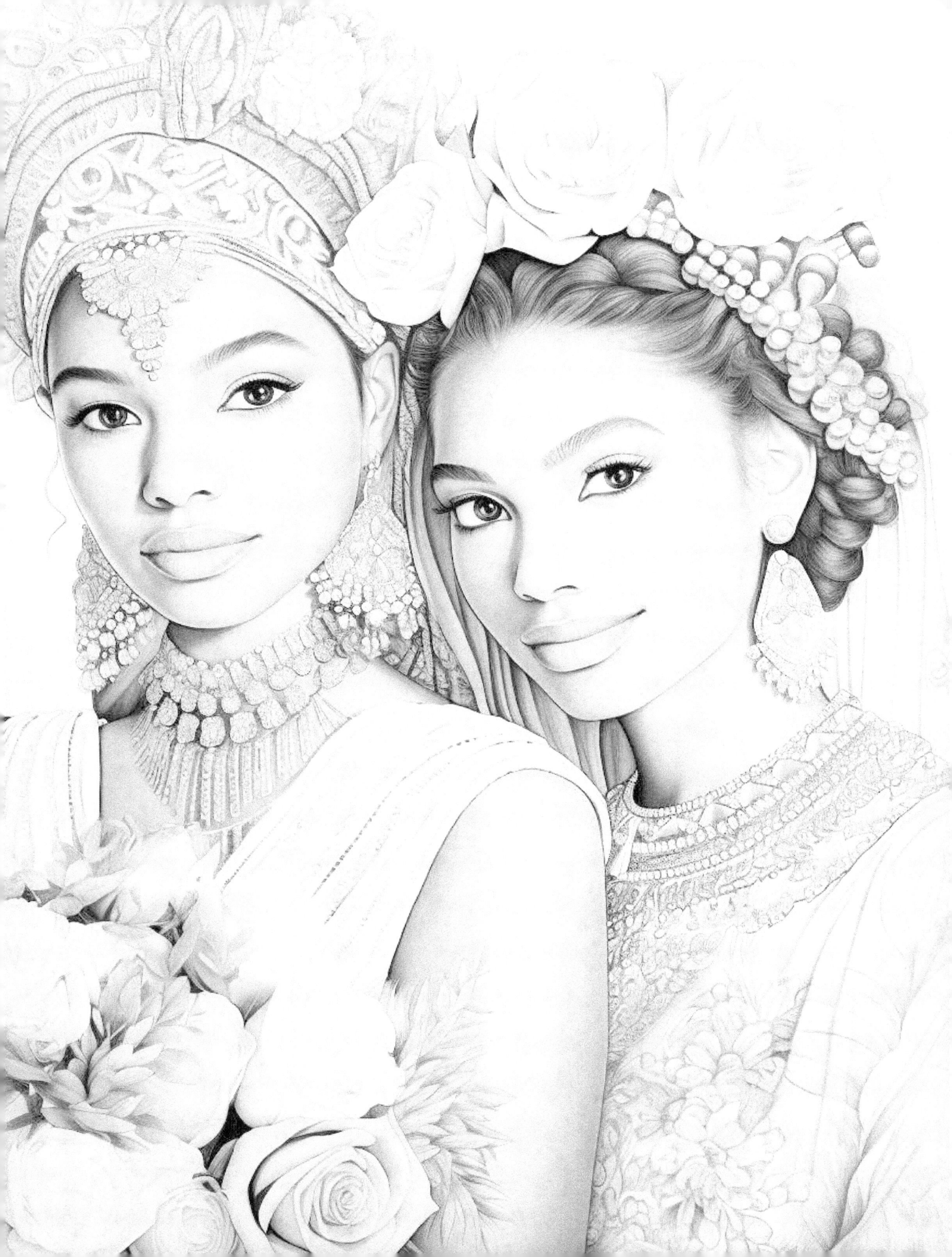

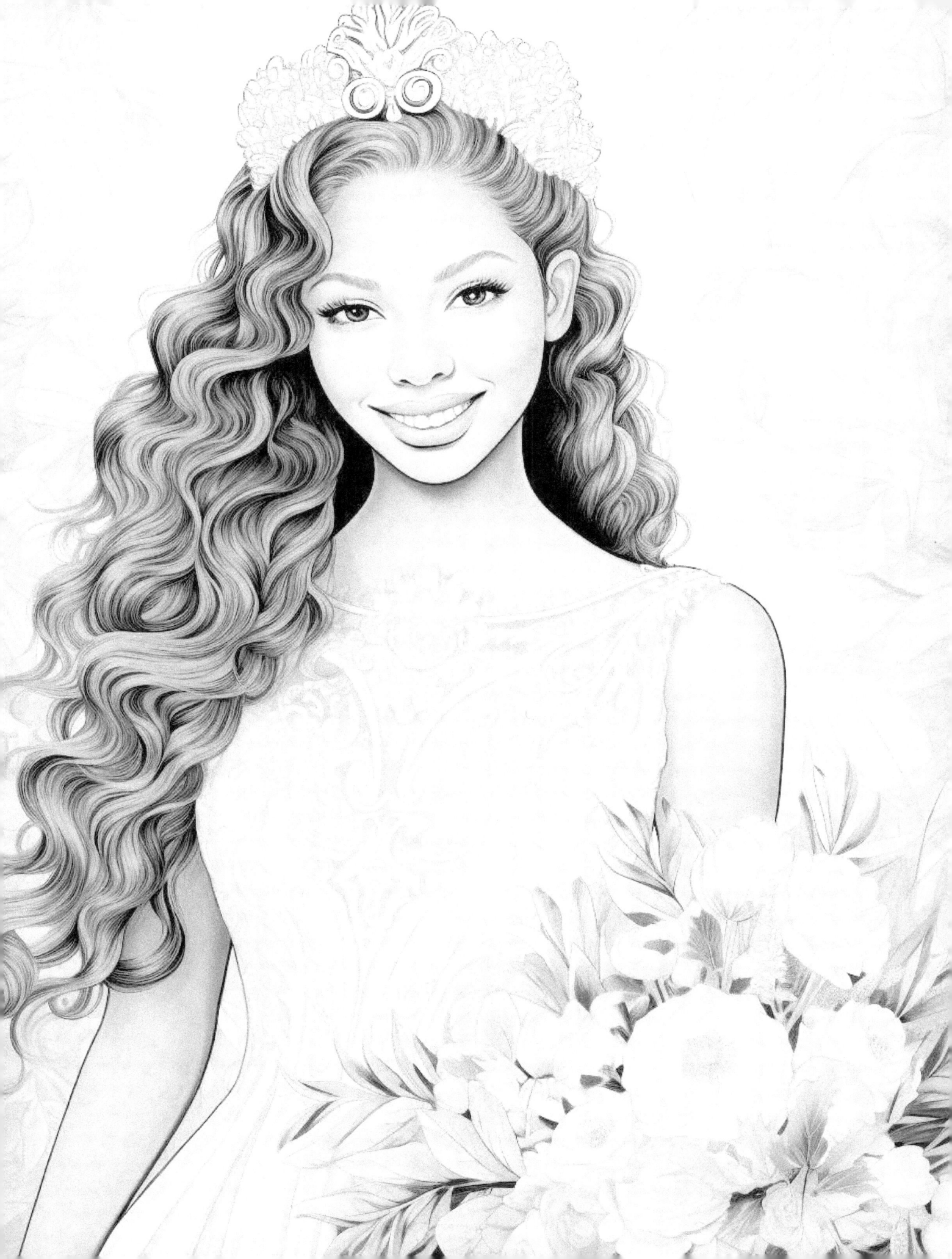

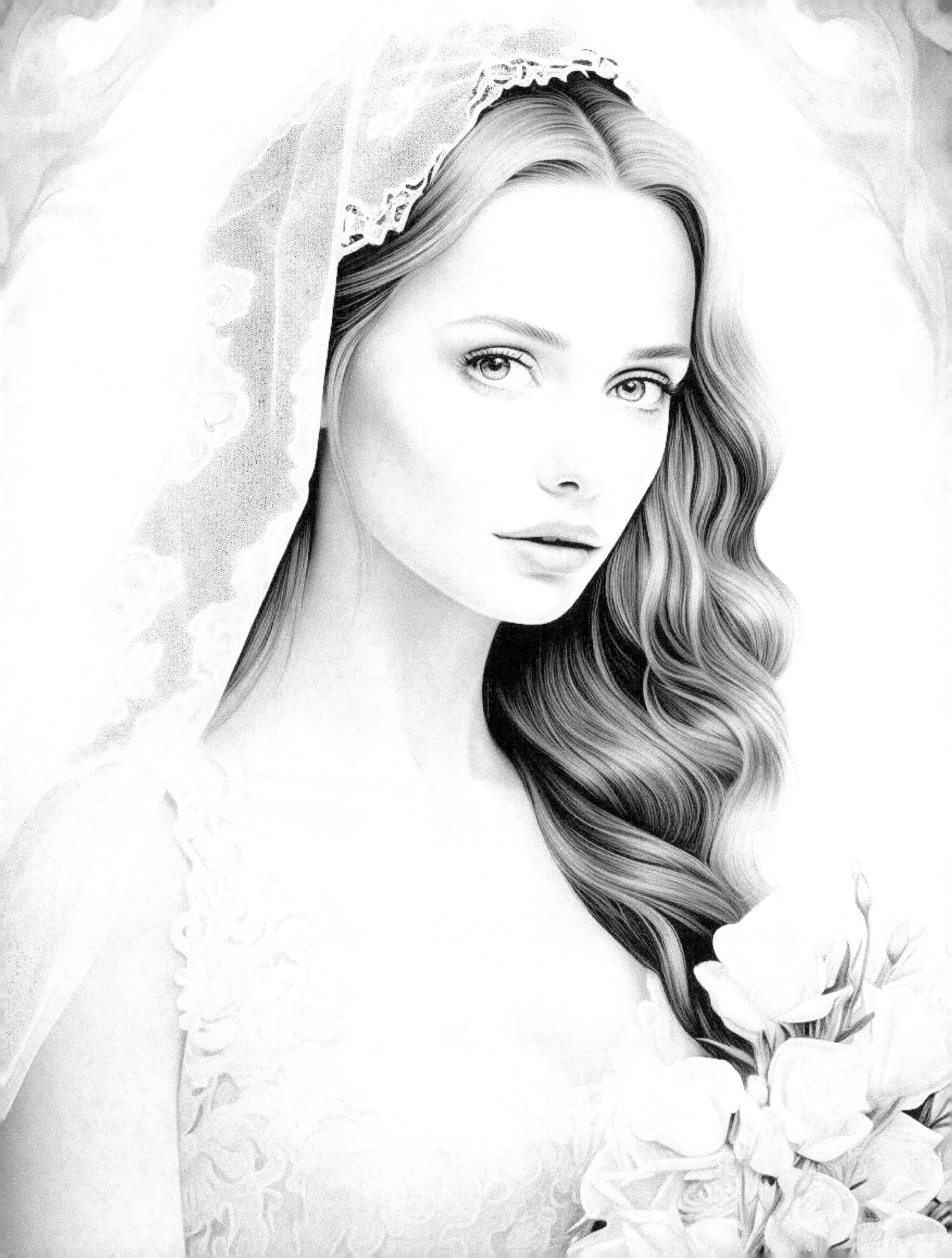

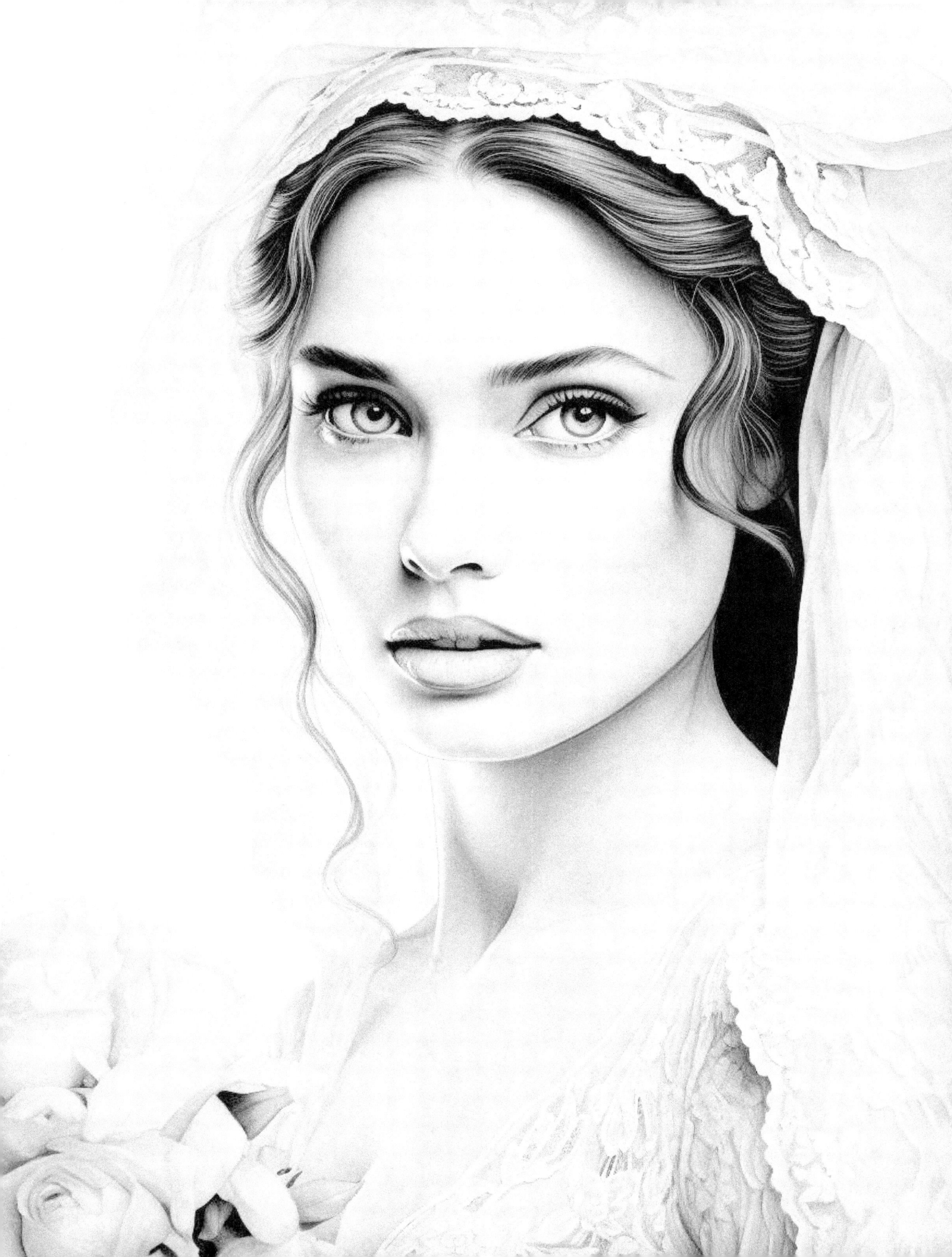

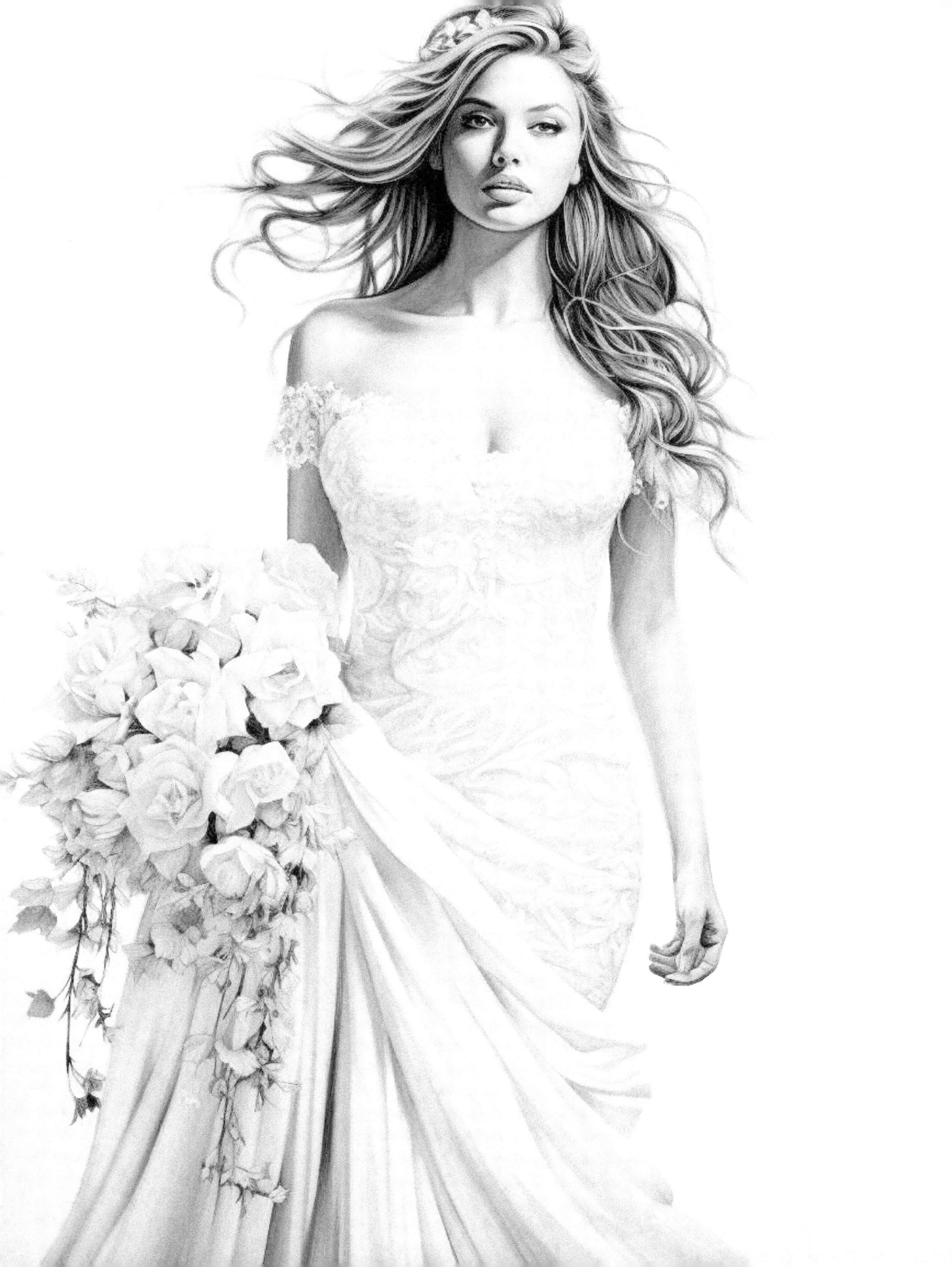

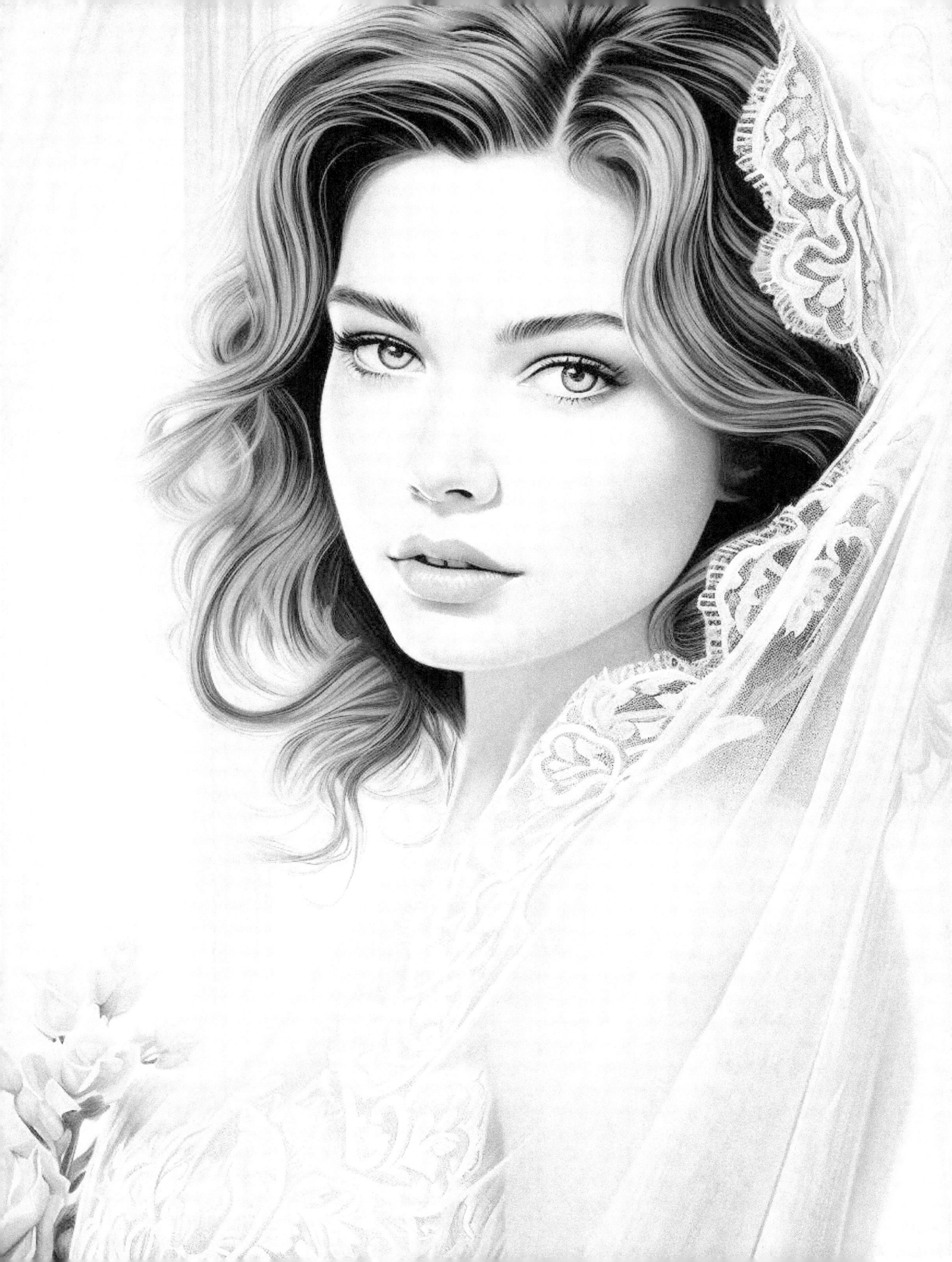

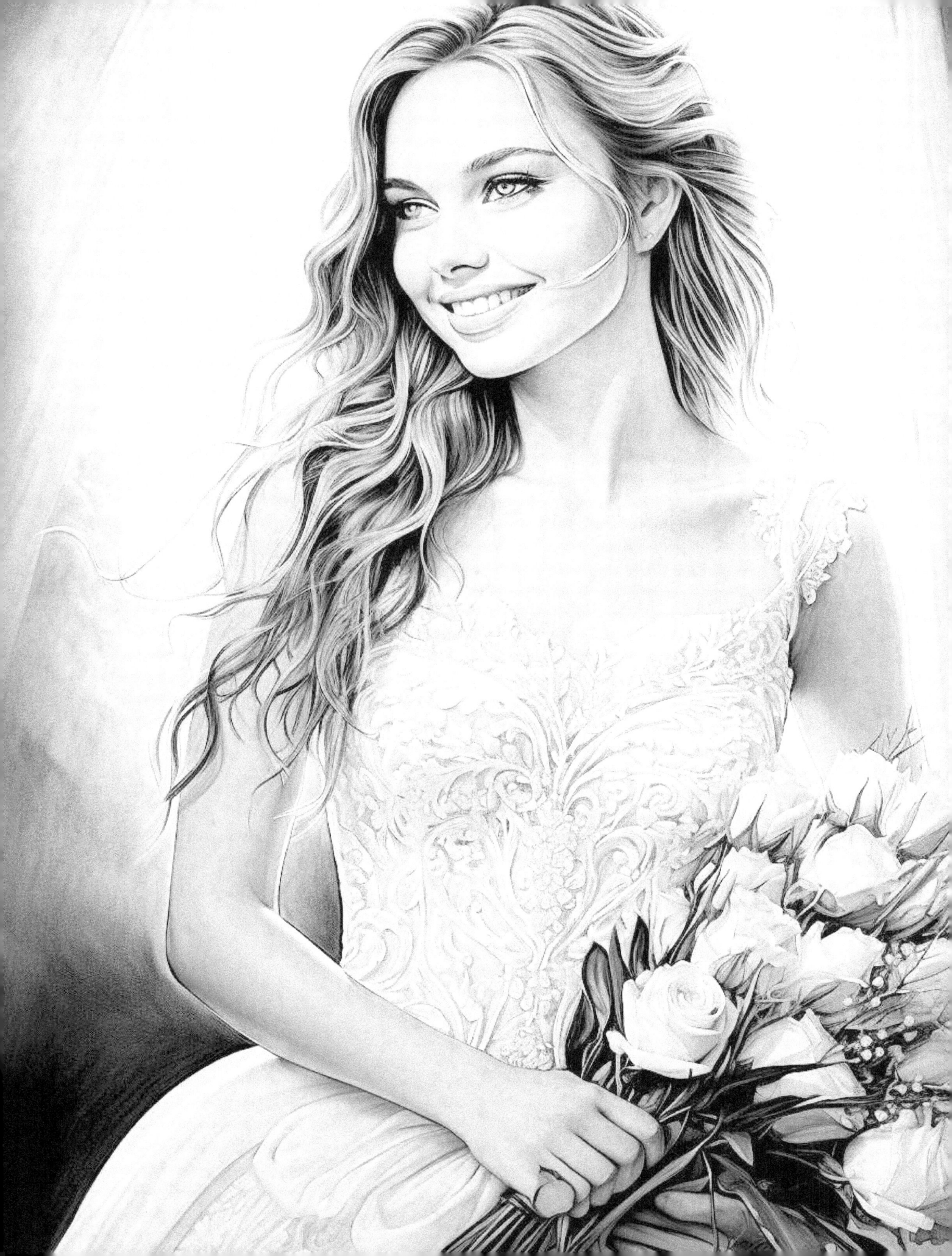

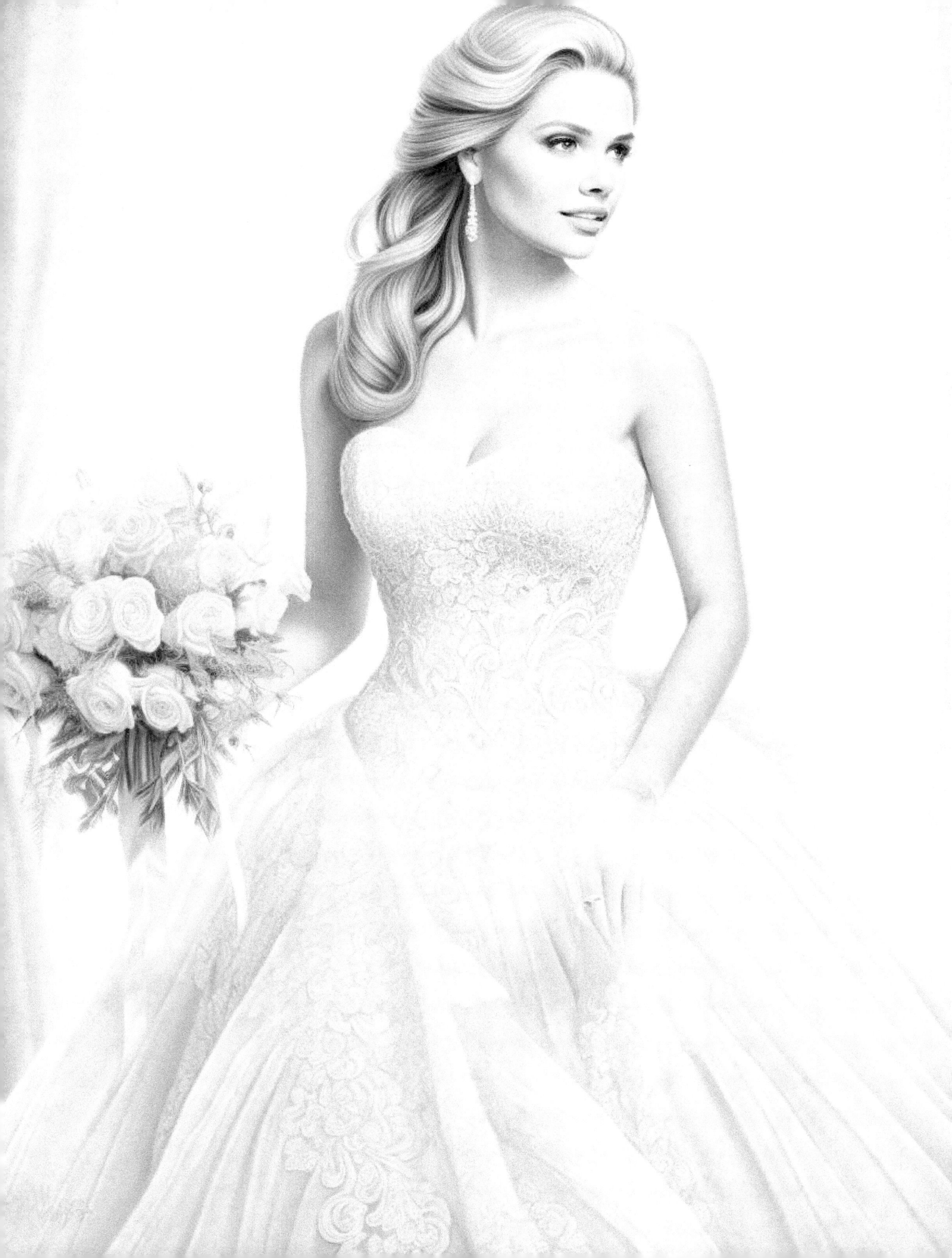

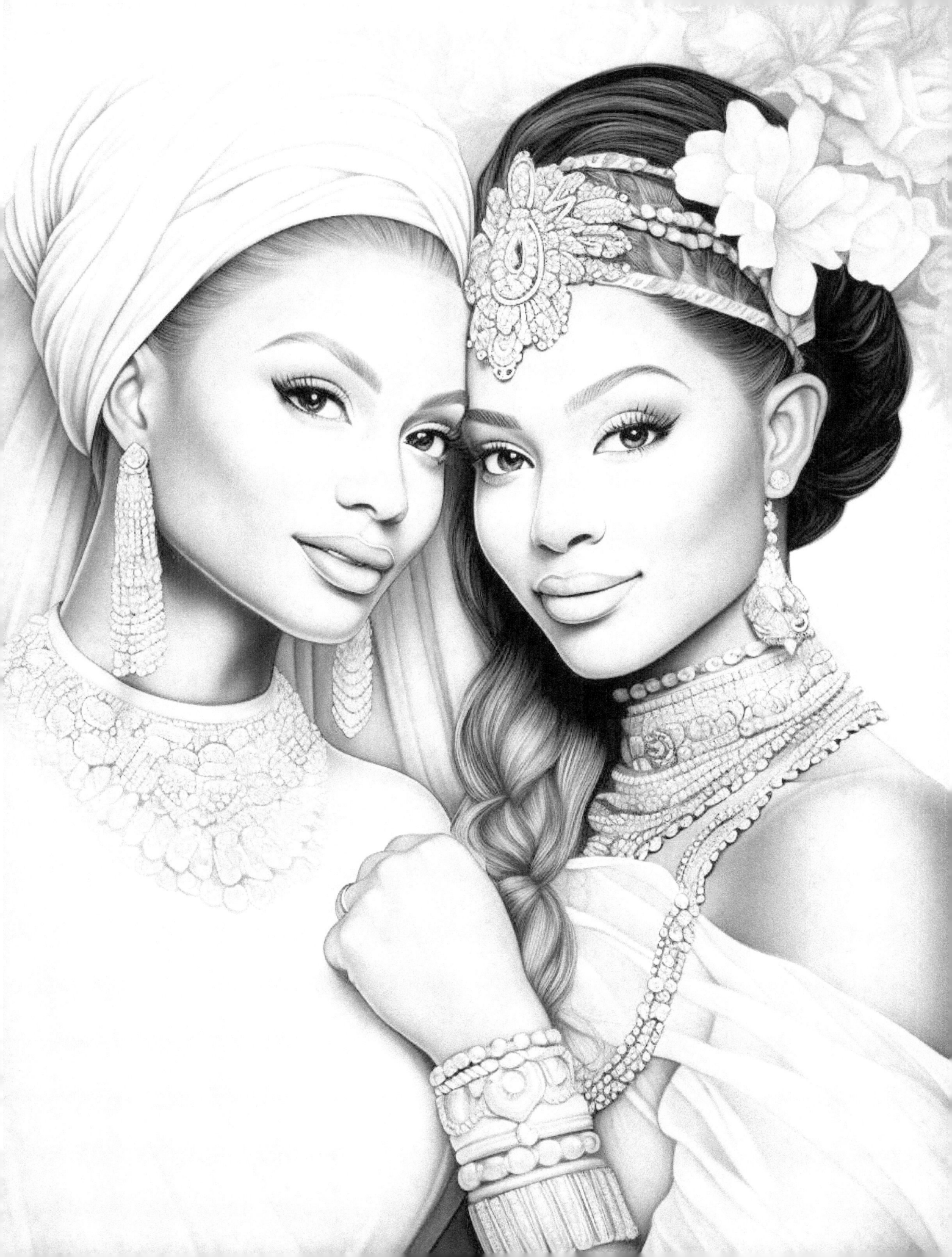

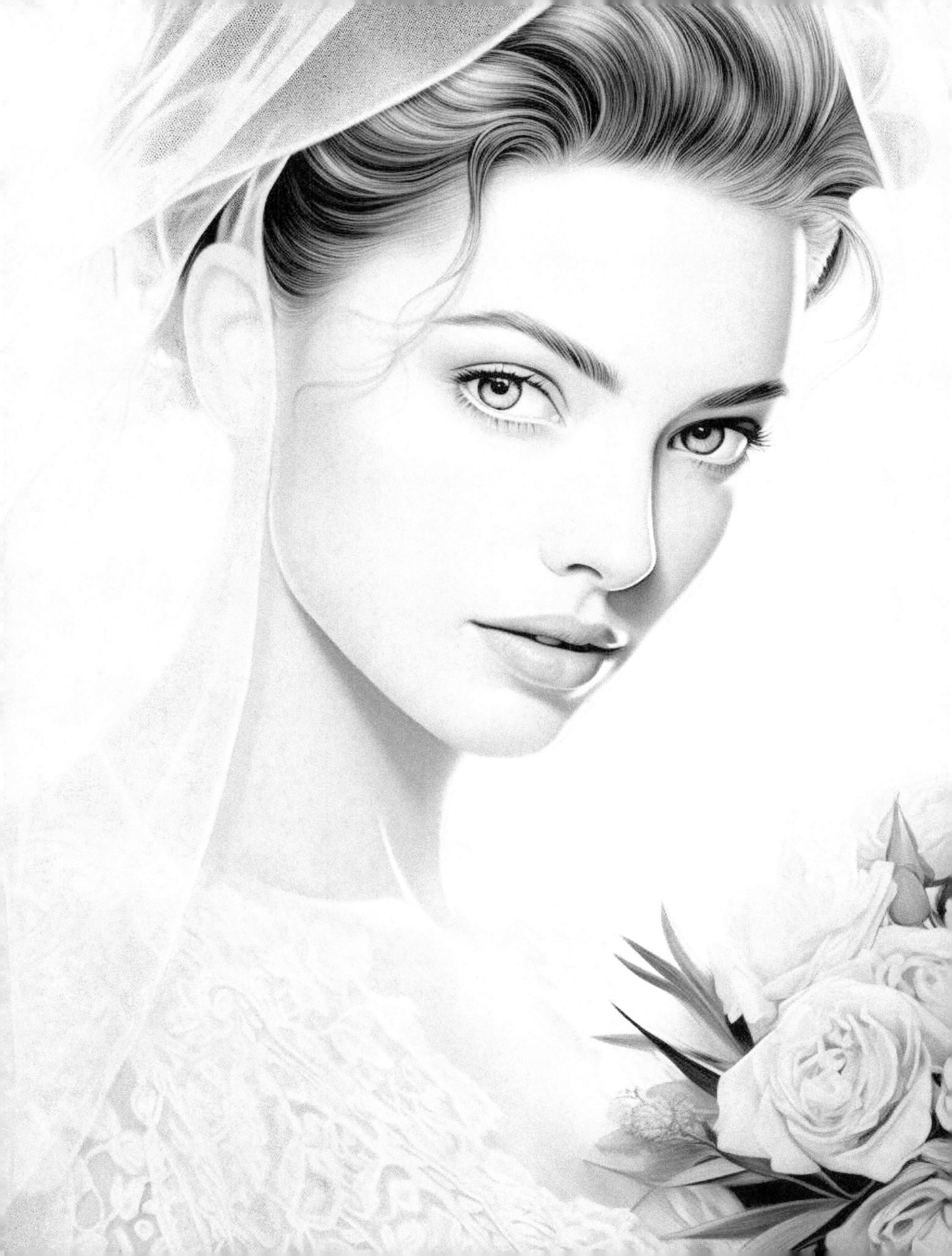

"If you enjoyed our product, it would be greatly appreciated if you could leave a review so others can receive the same benefits you have. Your review will help us see what is and what isn't working so we can serve you better and all our other customers even more."

For more beautiful books
Please scan the QR code to access
the Amazon page

**Fantasy Femmes:
Pretty Women's Portraits
Coloring Journey**

**Seasonal Women:
A Coloring Journey
Through the Seasons**

**Feminine Elegance Across
Cultures: A Timeless
Portrait Coloring Books**

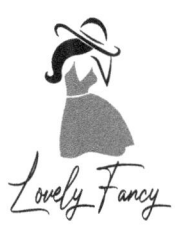

Lovely Fancy